FEED
ME

FEED ME

50 HOME COOKED MEALS FOR YOUR DOG

RECIPES AND TEXT BY
LIVIANA PROLA

HOW TO FEED YOUR DOG

The Rules

"You are what you eat," as the saying goes, and it's as true of dogs as it is of humans. The right diet for a dog is central to so many things; it helps them maintain healthy blood circulation, healthy muscle tone, and in building new tissue as he or she grows. Even better news is that feeding your dog the right food is quicker, simpler, and more cost effective than you might think. First, though, you need to get to grips with a few basics.

A dog's diet should follow some fundamental rules:

* it must be well balanced
* it must be easy for them to digest
* it must look, smell, and taste appetizing
* it must be full of dog-friendly ingredients

The right kind of diet should not only be satisfying, but also contain all the nutrients a dog needs to stay healthy—namely water, proteins, fats, minerals, and vitamins (for further reading, please see page 164). As with humans, it's about the perfect balance of the right ingredients—a good diet avoids anything in excess, and deficiency in any particular nutrient group. That means well-measured quantities of delicious ingredients, which is exactly what you will find in the recipes in this book.

Digestibility is also crucial when it comes to home-cooked food, and it depends not only on the ingredients themselves, but also on how they are prepared. In general, meat products are easiest for dogs to digest. Vegetables are a different story; they're high in fiber, so serve mainly to regulate intestinal function and bacterial flora found in the gut. Starch, such as that in cereals and potatoes, is easily digested by dogs when cooked and, unlike in humans, digestion only begins in dogs' intestines, making the process longer and more complex. In simple terms, that means that starch found in rice, potatoes, and pasta is only a valuable source of energy when it's been cooked for a long time— what would be deemed overdone for humans is just the right consistency for dogs.

How appetizing food will be to a dog couldn't be more important. We humans can decide to eat foods that we may not be fond of, but which we begrudgingly accept are necessary to eat because they are good for us—and we often take that ability for granted.

THE RULES

But like us, dogs don't all have the same tastes when it comes to what they like and don't like to eat. As a rule they prefer meat. Additionally, they prefer moist foods over dry, warm foods over cold, and if foods are fatty, so much the better. Perhaps unsurprisingly, the smell of the food is crucial. Dogs may not have many taste buds, but when it comes to smell, their abilities are unsurpassed—and so an appetizing smell plays a huge role in what they will happily eat.

Why Switch to Homemade Meals?

So why do people want to cook homemade meals for their dogs? There are a lot of reasons. For some, it's a decision based on quality—knowing that every mouthful will be the very best food it can be. For others, it's a way of monitoring portion control, or knowing that they are feeding their pet in the most appropriate way for its age and state of health. On top of that, the act of cooking for those you love—yes, even the dog—is satisfying in itself. Whatever the reason for taking this path, remember that it's an important choice, a gesture to which the proper care, attention, and time must be paid.

Drawing up a homemade meal plan that will meet the energy and nutritional requirements of a dog takes time; whether a lot or a little depends on the type of meal plan, and also on our individual cooking skills and the way we organize ourselves. In any case, the reality is that it will require more time than balancing store-bought, commercial pet food.

In short, it's not a decision to be taken lightly—you should always consult your dog's veterinarian before embarking on any change in diet—but, it does offer undeniable advantages, such as:

- more palatable food: normally, and regardless of size or breed, all dogs appreciate homemade meals
- no synthetic preservatives or antioxidants: preparing fresh food means it doesn't need to be stored for a long time, so no stabilizers are needed
- more protein: extrusion, the process used to make kibble (ground protein made into pellets, used in commercial dog food), requires a certain amount of starch to be added to the formula; this is something that isn't necessary in homemade meals, so they usually tend to contain more sources of protein with better nutritional values
- better digestibility
- higher-quality ingredients
- more flexibility in the choice of ingredients

Even overweight dogs or those with adverse reactions to foods can benefit greatly from home-cooked meals; the higher level of protein in homemade dog food (compared to kibble) can result in an increase of both the dog's lean body mass and its basic nutritional requirements. In the case of dogs with allergies, the advantage of more flexibility in your choice of ingredients means

HOW TO FEED YOUR DOG

that you can eliminate ingredients to monitor a difference in reactions—as it's impossible to control exactly what is in every commercially made meal. In homemade food, this is all within your control, and so an elimination diet can be trialled to find out exactly what is causing the reaction.

Even though home-cooked food provides flexibility, it's important to remember that this doesn't mean you can improvise—you'll need to follow the recipes and their instructions, and, as previously stated, always consult your veterinarian before embarking on switching to homemade meals, to make sure it's the right decision for your pet. Follow the recipes to the letter: if a food plan takes into account, for example, the nutritional values of beef loin (from an animal 12-18 months old), you mustn't use another cut of meat. Ingredients in recipes for humans may be very similar nutritionally, but, in a dog's diet, it has to be calculated much more carefully. So if you can't source the right ingredients, think about trying another recipe first—with 50 meals to choose from, there are plenty of options that range in ease. Changing food is inevitably going to be a delicate thing for a dog—even a switch in brand can cause some of them to turn their noses up—and that can also be the case when transitioning from commercial products to a homemade diet. The reasons for this aren't clear, but the simple fact is that dry commercial dog food has been standardized, and therefore is utterly consistent. A dog that's been fed kibble for years has developed very specific intestinal flora. Introducing a wider and more complex range of ingredients means that the dog's intestinal flora has to be able to diversify. So in practical terms, what does that mean? Dogs and their stomachs are creatures of habits, so any changes need to be introduced slowly, to allow their bodies to adjust to it.

How to Move to a Homemade Diet

The transition from a commercial diet to a homemade one should always be gradual. So, to completely exclude kibble from your dog's diet, you'll need to take your time, meal by meal, over the course of at least two weeks.

Here are some simple ratios to follow, using the meals in this book. You'll need to calculate the percentage of the correct portion size for your dog, as stated in each recipe:

DIET SWITCH TIME PLAN

	COMMERCIAL DIET	HOMEMADE DIET
THE FIRST 5 DAYS	Reduce by 25%	add half of the amount of protein (meat or fish) specified in the recipe
DAYS 5-10	Reduce by 50%	add half of the amount of protein (meat or fish), and half of the vegetables specified in the recipe
DAYS 10-15	Reduce by 75%	add half of the amount of protein (meat or fish), half of the vegetables, and all of the oils specified in the recipe
DAY 15	Feed your dog the homemade food exclusively	

Following on from this, you can feed your dog exclusively homemade food. If, during the transition to home-cooked food, your dog develops any kind of digestive problems, it's a good idea to extend the first step of this time plan for as long as necessary. Of course, if this doesn't stop, then you should seek advice from your veterinarian.

Should this be the case, try one of the recipes that includes a fermented milk product, such as yogurt or kefir, for 3-5 days (or until the problem has disappeared) and then continue with the transition.

WHEN SHOULD YOU START TO FEED YOUR DOG HOMEMADE FOOD?

The right time to introduce homemade food into your dog's diet is a much-debated topic, especially in the case of growing puppies. Young dogs have very specific nutritional requirements (see page 164 onwards for more information), but this doesn't mean you can't move a pup to a homemade diet as soon as it has been weaned from its mother's milk—unless there are specific health conditions that you are aware of.

A newly-weaned puppy's gastrointestinal tract is still immature, as is its intestinal flora. This means that the foods it's given at this stage must be easily digestible; plant-based proteins (peas, soybeans, green beans, etc.) must therefore be avoided, as must sources of insoluble fiber (carrots, leafy greens, squash, zucchini (courgette). What should, however, be included immediately after weaning are meat and eggs. You'll find three great recipes for puppies in this book that are an excellent starting point (see page 44 onwards).

WHAT HAPPENS IF YOU NEED TO TAKE A BREAK FROM COOKING?

Over the course of a year, there may be times when it is not easy to cook your dog's food with the usual care and regularity. This can happen when traveling, for instance. The simplest solution in such a case would be to return to a commercial diet for a short time, following the time plan on page 15 in reverse order from homemade food to commercial food. Often, however, dogs are not very happy with this arrangement, and don't accept the change that willingly. However, with a little advanced planning, you can follow tips for storing and freezing that will minimise the impact on your dog's diet (see page 34 and 37). That said, it is always a good idea to consult your veterinary nutritionist before giving your dog a mixed diet.

Foods to Include

MEAT

Meat is the favorite food of dogs—the majority of them, anyway. It's certainly one of most widely used ingredients in their food. The best meats to cook with are chicken, turkey, beef, and lamb, but also some cuts of pork, such as loin or (defatted) leg work well for dogs. This is because lean meats with little connective tissue are higher in good-quality protein and are also more digestible. However, meat is low in some minerals, such as calcium, and some vitamins. Over-consumption of meat can lead to uncomfortable fermentation in the intestines and flatulence.

Bones deserve a special mention. Naturally, dogs and wolves are always hungry for them; this is because they're an important source of calcium. In a homemade diet, though, it's better to avoid the use of whole bones because they're potentially dangerous for dogs to consume; once cooked, they can splinter as the dog eats them and damage their throats and stomachs. Try bone meal or supplements as an alternative source of calcium that's much easier to control the quantity.

FISH

Oily fish, hake, cod, sole, or plaice, and freshwater fish such as salmon and trout, are excellent ingredients for your dog's food. As we know, fish is high in good-quality proteins, essential amino acids, fatty acids such as omega 3, and minerals. Again, the important thing is to cook it well. Although compared to meat there is a much lower risk of contracting viruses, such as Aujezsky's disease, and bacteria, several common species of fish contain an enzyme called thiaminase, which is able to block the absorption of vitamin B1, which can affect your dog's metabolism of carbohydrates, fats and proteins—all essential for your dog's organs to function properly.

EGGS

Eggs, containing all the essential amino acids, are a very digestible source of protein with a high nutritional value.

MILK AND OTHER DAIRY PRODUCTS

When it comes to dairy products, it's all about choosing ingredients with the right lactose levels. Although milk is a complete food from a nutritional point of view, in a homemade dog food diet it's not used much because of the lactose it contains; this sugar is not good for adult dogs because they don't have the enzyme (lactase) necessary for digesting it (see the section on food intolerances on page 194). Among other dairy products, however, there are a number are that are completely lactose-free, or contain very low levels, so are therefore suitable for dogs. Aged cheeses, such as Parmigiano Reggiano or Grana Padano) and Cheddar, for example, contain minimal amounts of lactose, and are all great sources of protein. Dairy products such as ricotta, and kefir, are very low in lactose and can help to strengthen the immune system. Butter, too, is good for dogs, because it's a very easily digestible fat. To avoid problems, the rule is not to overdo it, because generally a small amount of lactose won't lead to any signs of intolerance.

OFFAL

There are many by-products of butchering that can be included in your dog's diet, which are a great bolster for other sources of protein. Among the most commonly used are hearts, lungs, kidneys, spleens, and tripe, which, although they are often considered waste products, are full of vitamins and protein. Pork and chicken offal, as with all meat from pigs and chickens, should be well cooked. Liver should always be given in the quantities recommended in these recipes, or those suggested by your veterinarian or a veterinary nutritionist, in order to to avoid an accumulation of vitamins A and D, which can be harmful over time.

FRUIT AND VEGETABLES

With the exception of onions and garlic—which are toxic to dogs—any kind of vegetable can be included in a dog's diet.

What matters with fruit and vegetables is what your dog likes. The most popular ingredients with dogs are usually carrots, squash, and zucchini (courgettes). Fennel, chard, celery, lettuce leaves of various kinds, and other leafy greens, as well as spinach, and beets (beetroot), peppers, tomatoes, and eggplants (aubergine) when cooked are used less, not because there are medical side effects, but because dogs generally don't like them. Broccoli, cauliflower, cabbage, and spinach, used frequently, can lead to calcium metabolism and oxalate problems.

The fruit that dogs like most are apples, apricots, and peaches, which are good sources of vitamins and antioxidants. Grapes should not be included because they're toxic, and it's not advisable to give them bananas as they're hard for dogs to digest.

Again, though, it's important to not overdo fruit and vegetable intake. Too much fiber can be a cause of intestinal disorders and, in the long run, can also cause a weakening of their coat. As with humans, moderation is key.

OILS AND FATS

Dogs can eat oils and fat that derive from both animals and plants. Among the former are fish oil (salmon and herring being the most common), krill oil, butter, and lard. The latter include wheat germ oil, almond oil, corn oil, sunflower oil, and many others, all of which are very easily digested. Some plant-based oils also contain vitamin E, the most powerful natural antioxidant. For dogs, vitamin E is essential for a thick, shiny, healthy coat, and can be included in their diet as a supplement. However, if it's obtained from plant-based oils, it's absorbed better, and this means the amount included in their diet can be less—so if a recipe specifies an animal or plant oil or fat, then don't deviate from that, it's for good reason. Extra-virgin olive oil is not necessarily the best choice for your dog: its intense flavor often makes food unappetizing to them but, above all, extra-virgin olive oil has an essential fatty acid content that's lower than that of corn, sunflower or peanut oil (high in omega 6) but also that of soy, flaxseed (linseed) or canola oil. Essential fatty acids, together with zinc, are the nutrients which are best for the good health of your dog's skin. Coconut oil is also really good, in particular for senior dogs, and is easily digested.

CEREALS, BREADS, POTATOES, AND PSEUDOCEREALS

In the context of carbohydrate, the main energy sources for dogs are found in cereals, bread, root vegetables, and cooked legumes. Of cereals, rice is most digestible, but dogs also like cereal flakes (corn, wheat, barley, and oat), puffed rice, and pre-cooked pasta. As all of these come pre-cooked, they can be heated through after being rehydrated in warm water. If your dog has a cereal intolerance, good alternatives are root vegetables, potatoes, and tapioca in particular, and legumes such as peas, although this is quite an uncommon condition. Then there are pseudocereals such as amaranth and quinoa, which are an important source of carbohydrate and protein.

SEAWEED

This is an important source of trace elements (selenium, iodine, zinc) but it also contains fatty acids (especially omega 3) and protein. Among the varieties suitable for dogs are spirulina (spirulina platensis) and kelp (macrocistis pyrifera). Both improve the appearance of a dog's coat and will contribute nutrients to their nervous systems. The addition of seaweed to your dog's diet means you can spend less on commercial supplements, although you will need to monitor the amount of iodine.

SUPERFOODS

Superfoods are high in nutrients such as vitamins, minerals, essential fatty acids, and antioxidants—they're as good a dietary boost for dogs as they are for humans. Antioxidants are among the most beneficial nutrients because they're able to neutralize free radicals and protect the body from their negative actions. Furthermore, they're true "scavengers", eliminating the waste that cells leave behind. In short, antioxidants can slow the process of cellular degeneration that causes aging, and can thus be held as 'elixirs of life' in both human and veterinary medicine. There are lots of ingredients included in this food group, such as ginger, turmeric, rosemary, goji berries, and cranberries, which you'll find in a lot of the recipes, however, it's important to remember that these should also be consumed in moderation.

→ IN BRIEF

- → Proteins are the basis of dogs' diets
- → Fats are a great source of energy
- → Vitamins and minerals must always be added to home-cooked meals
- → The main form of digestible carbohydrate for dogs is starch, found in bread, rice, grains, and legumes
- → Dogs should drink 3½ tablespoons/50ml water per 2 lb/1 kg body weight a day

HOW TO MOVE TO A HOMEMADE DIET

HOW TO FEED YOUR DOG

Foods to Avoid

Of course, there are foods that should always be avoided in your dog's diet—some ingredients can have problematic, long-term effects on the health of your dog, and even more serious consequences. To find a full list of these ingredients, please visit the recommended websites in the back of this book, however, here we've provided a list of the most common foods consumed by humans that people can often think are ok to feed their pets. A classic example? Chocolate—just because it's a great treat for us, it doesn't mean it's a great treat for dogs, as it can cause symptoms such as an upset stomach.

<u>WHICH FOODS ARE TOXIC?</u>

One of the first steps on the path to a homemade diet for dogs is to understand that some foods—normally present in our kitchens—and integral parts of our daily diets, are absolutely poisonous to dogs and must never be put in their food bowl. These include the following:

- Onions, garlic, etc.
- Grapes
- Macadamia nuts
- Chocolate, coffee, and tea
- Avocado

Of course, none of these ingredients are used in these recipes, but it's good to have the information on hand. For more detailed information, plus further reading, please see page 164 onward.

In nature, there are also some plants (for example, oleanders, orchids, fig trees, poinsettias) that are toxic and even deadly for dogs, but they have not been further discussed, for the reasons mentioned above.

Managing Meals

One of the most common questions is how many meals a dog should eat each day. The answer is that, generally, for an adult dog it's best to divide the day's portion of food into two meals: one in the morning, the other in the evening. This is for three reasons: the first is to avoid your dog eating too much in one go. If you think about it, this is the same reason why it's best for us to separate meals—if a dog eats only once a day, the meal would have to be very generous and, because they wouldn't have eaten for twenty four hours, they would be ravenous.

Secondly, digestion burns a certain amount of the body's energy, and so splitting the meals is a useful way of keeping your dog's weight under control, especially if they need to trim down.

The third reason is psychological. Dogs are always looking for extra food and, as we well know, are pretty good at making it impossible to say 'no' to them. Portioning a dog's daily diet into two meals makes it easier for both them and us. If you really want to give your dog a snack, though, then the best way to do this is to remove the fruit, vegetables, or yogurt from one of the recipes, and reserve them as snacks—helpful for when they are giving you puppy eyes while you are eating your own meals. It also means that you are still in full control of their diet, and not accidentally giving them more than they need. So when using this book, remember that the daily portion is for the full day— you don't need to double it if you are feeding your dog twice. Remember too, that if you plan to take your dog for a long walk, you should wait at least four hours from when it has eaten before setting off. Finally, you should never leave food around to eat at any time it likes, but it's vital to have a bowl of fresh, clean water available always.

WHY YOU SHOULD VARY YOUR DOG'S DIET

There is a fundamental difference in the importance of a varied diet for dogs and humans. For humans, variety equates to a balanced diet, and one that allows us to take in all the nutrients that our body needs, in the right amounts. Conversely, a dog can get all the nutrients it needs by eating the same foods every day. Its entire diet, in fact, is balanced over a single day: this means that each of its meals already contains all the proteins, fats, vitamins, and minerals that it needs to stay happy and healthy.

MANAGING MEALS

However, giving a dog a varied diet is good for other reasons. Just like us, they can get bored of eating the same thing too often, and so feeding them different meals is a great way of stimulating their appetite and keeping them interested in their food, as opposed to what you have on the table for yourself.

As the recipes in this book are all perfectly balanced nutritionally, you could pick and choose what to cook, and how often to vary the meals, depending on what particular flavors your dog enjoys.

Food Prep and Cooking

By far, the best way to cook dog food is to steam the ingredients—that way, you don't need any additional oils or fats to cook it, and you can guarantee the food is perfectly balanced. To do this, you just need to boil some water in the bottom of a normal saucepan into which a basket or a colander containing the ingredients you want to cook is placed. The food shouldn't be immersed in the boiling water, just suspended over the steam; this will ensure that most of the food's smell and taste are preserved and allows it to absorb moisture and other aromas, but not lose any of its inherent goodness. A great tip is to reserve the cooking water—you can add it to the dog's food to make it softer and more palatable, and even better, you're adding any lost nutrients back into the food.

BASIC RULES FOR COOKING INGREDIENTS

From a purely nutritional point of view, raw meat is preferable: cooking actually depletes nutrients, in particular vitamins in meat. This isn't applicable for all meat, though—for example, chicken and turkey, which can contain high levels of bacterial contamination (salmonella, listeria, campylobacter, etc.), are only microbiologically safe after cooking. Even pork (and wild boar) is only safe when it's been cooked all the way through. That's because it can contain the Aujeszky disease virus, which is the cause of the disease of the same name—also known as pseudorabies—that is fatal to dogs but not transmissable to humans. So the golden rule is, follow the recipes to the letter—if it's suggested that meat is cooked, there's good reason for it. Finally, make sure that all the long bones have been removed from chicken, turkey, and rabbit because, when chewed, these can break into sharp splinters and cause injuries to your dog. In addition, bones can cause obstructions in the dog's intestines, and a rapid deterioration of a dog's teeth. Ground bone meal, however, is safe to use.

Fish must always be cooked, taking care to remove all the bones.

Eggs should always be soft-boiled so that the white is cooked and the yolk remains runny.

Carbohydrates, such as cereals (rice and pasta, for example), and potatoes, require a longer cooking time than you would prepare them for your own meals. In fact, on average, cereals will need to be cooked for around five minutes longer that what is indicated on the package. As for potatoes, before being eaten they should be boiled for a long time and then puréed. If you don't have potato, or your dog doesn't like it, an excellent substitute is tapioca. Tapioca flour can be used to make mush or be shaped into fingers, while tapioca pearls or flakes can be rehydrated in water before being cooked.

Finally, as a general rule, fresh, well-washed vegetables can be eaten raw to best preserve the nutrients (especially vitamins) that are partially lost in cooking. Raw vegetables often aren't a dog's favorite part of the meal—steaming softens them and makes it easy to mix them with meat or fish so your dog can't avoid eating them. But, if your dog really can't abide them, try blending them so they go under the radar. Remember that squash and eggplants (aubergines) must always be cooked, and so must legumes (e.g. peas, green beans, and soybeans).

HOW TO FEED YOUR DOG

Serving the Meal

At the point of serving food, it's important that all the ingredients are really well mixed. As previously suggested, combining some of the cooking water with the solid food makes it softer and easier to wolf down, which your dog will appreciate.

In general, oils and fats should always be added cold, at the end, when the food has been cooked. The same goes for supplements.

Salt deserves a special mention. The sodium requirement for dogs is normally met by the ingredients present in their diet; it isn't necessary to add salt to the food of healthy dogs. In animals who have bladder stones, however, you will need to consult your veterinarian, if this is the case.

Finally, meals should always be served warm. Dogs aren't partial to cold food, and hot food—if the dog is particularly hungry—can cause serious burns to its mouth and throat. Be as careful as possible if you are using the microwave to warm the food, as the center of it—especially if it contains water—can be hotter than the outer parts.

THE DINING EXPERIENCE

The choice of bowl is also important. It should be of stainless steel, preferably, as this is a material which, compared to others, is more hygienic and easier to clean, sturdy, and has no nooks and crannies that can accumulate residue and lead to the spread of fungi and bacteria. You should also choose the bowl according to the size of your dog and its nose. For example, a dog with a pronounced nose that's medium to large in size will find it easier to eat from a higher, narrower bowl, while a dog with a short nose, such as a Boxer, Bulldog, or Pug, will find it easier to use a low, wide bowl so that it won't get dirty while it's eating.

If you have more than one dog, it's a good idea to place the bowls at a distance from each other, preferably in different areas. This avoids the dogs eating too quickly for fear that the other dogs might eat their food and also to stop them trying to eat the other dogs' food. Both things are dangerous—the dogs might fight, and it becomes hard to know how much any dog has actually eaten.

Storing Food

One of the biggest obstacles on the path to a homemade diet is time. But there are tips that can help simplify matters and avoid you spending entire evenings in the kitchen. In fact, you don't need to cook every day: you can do it in advance and refrigerate or freeze individual foods in ready-to-eat portions. Remember though, that you should always cook fresh food: food that's been kept in the freezer already must never be refrozen.

HOW TO STORE INDIVIDUAL INGREDIENTS

Meat and fish for example, once cooked, can be frozen, refrigerated, or vacuum-packed. In the refrigerator they can be stored for three to four days, or vacuum-sealed, and then refrigerated up to seven days. You can keep them in the freezer for about three months.

Boiled eggs can last in the refrigerator for up to a week, but they must be chilled within two hours of cooking. It's best to avoid storing them in the freezer as the consistency of egg white changes.

When refrigerated, carbohydrates can form resistant starch (RS). Before refrigerating or freezing them, it's a good idea to wash them to avoid this. Potatoes should be cooked as needed each day, and eaten by your dog before they have cooled completely.

Cooked vegetables should be stored in glass containers or plastic bags in the refrigerator for no longer than two to three days; if you want to freeze them, it's a good idea to dry them with paper towels then put them in plastic freezer bags: they can then be kept for up to 10 months.

Keep the time to a minimum between preparing the food and freezing it to avoid the spread of bacteria (this rule also applies when refrigerating): the trick is to divide the food into small portions so that they cool faster, and then store them in airtight containers or plastic food bags. At this point, run everything under cold running water, or, better still, place it in a container filled with ice, and allow water to flow over it until the food reaches room temperature, then dry the container and put everything in the freezer (or the refrigerator).

Store food that's to be frozen in plastic bags or special containers and affix a label stating what the food is and the date on which it was frozen: this way you will avoid leaving the food in the freezer for too long (and won't mix up your own portion of lasagne with your dog's food!)

The defrosting process should always be gradual: it's best to transfer the frozen food from the freezer to the refrigerator where the bacteria are less active than on the kitchen counter. This applies in particular to perishable foods such as meat and fish.

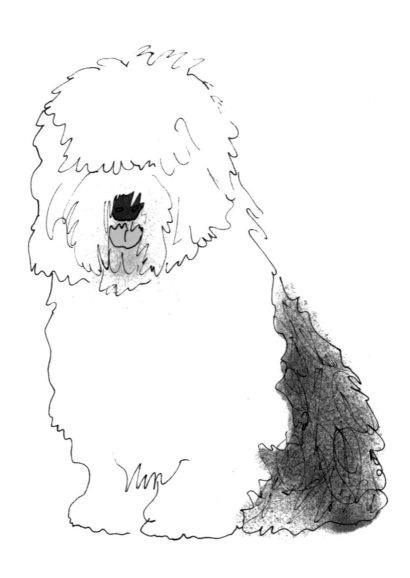

ABOUT THE RECIPES

How to Use the Recipes

The recipes in this book all take less than 40 minutes to prepare, and can be stored in the fridge for up to three to four days, and in the freezer for up to three months. You'll find more detailed information on how to store food on page 34. Ingredients can all be sourced from your butcher or supermarket, however, some offal might be a little trickier to find. In these instances, do not substitute ingredients—there are plenty that call for cuts of meat that are easily sourced. Every recipe has an easy-to-follow legend showing the predominant ingredient and dietary requirements, such as lighter recipes for dogs who need to slim down, to protein-rich dishes for active dogs.

Each meal gives a suggested serving size of cooked food based on the weight of your dog, along with a calorie count per 3½ ounces (100 g). You'll find a more detailed nutritional breakdown for each recipe in the Nutritional Values section, from page 124. In regards to this, all recipes are based on the requirements of a neutered dog. Please see page 207 for more details.

RECIPE LEGEND

RED MEAT—recipes include beef, lamb, or pork
POULTRY—recipes include chicken or duck
VEGETABLES—recipes with no meat, but do contain dairy
FISH—recipes containing fish or seafood
GAME—recipes including game, such as venison
VEGAN—recipes that contain no meat, eggs, or dairy
GRAIN FREE—recipes that contain no wheat or gluten
ENERGETIC—protein-rich recipes for active or working dogs
LIGHT—lighter dishes for older, less active, or overweight dogs

A NOTE ON WEIGHTS

These recipes were created using metric grams, so for accuracy, these measurements should be followed. However U.S. cups and ounces are also included.

A NOTE ON SUPPLEMENTS

Each recipe contains recommended shop-bought supplements to ensure your dog's nutritional needs are all met. We highly recommend that these are measured in grams, to ensure accuracy. You'll find more information on page 208.

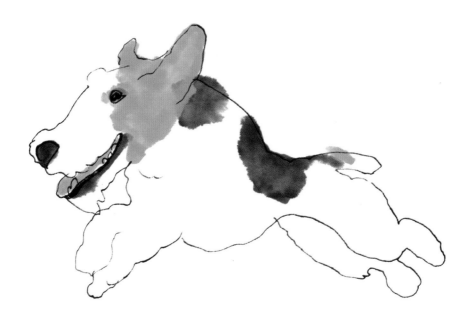

HOW TO USE THE RECIPES

RED MEAT

POULTRY

VEGETABLES

FISH

VEGAN

GRAIN FREE

ENERGETIC

GAME

LIGHT

PUPPIES

Carrot Risotto with Seared Beef

INGREDIENTS

2 LB 3¼ OZ/1 KG OF FOOD

White rice	1 cup/185 g
Carrots, sliced	1 cup/115 g
Lean beef, chopped	17 oz/485 g
Beef spleen, chopped	5¾ oz/165 g
Salmon oil	½ tbsp
Flaxseed (linseed) oil	1 ¼ tbsp
Supplement (page 208)	3 tbsp/23 g

WEIGHT OF ADULT: 6 LB 10 OZ/3 KG

WEIGHT OF PUPPY	MEAL SIZE
1 lb 2 oz (0.5 kg)	3 oz/85 g
2 lb 3¼ oz (1 kg)	4½ oz/130 g
4 lb 6 oz (2 kg)	6¼ oz/175 g

WEIGHT OF ADULT: 22 LB/10 KG

WEIGHT OF PUPPY	MEAL SIZE
6 lb 10 oz (3 kg)	11 oz/310 g
13¼ lb (6 kg)	15⅜ oz/435 g
20 lb (9 kg)	1 lb ¾ oz/475 g

WEIGHT OF ADULT: 55 LB/25 KG

WEIGHT OF PUPPY	MEAL SIZE
11 lb (5 kg)	15⅛ oz/430 g
22 lb (10 kg)	1 lb 5½ oz/610 g
33 lb (15 kg)	1 lb 10 ⅝ oz/755 g
44 lb (20 kg)	1 lb 10¼ oz/745 g

WEIGHT OF ADULT: 88 LB/40 KG

WEIGHT OF PUPPY	MEAL SIZE
11 lb (5 kg)	15⅛ oz/430 g
22 lb (10 kg)	1½ lb/680 g
33 lb (15 kg)	1 lb 13¾ oz/830 g
44 lb (20 kg)	2 lb 1½ oz/950 g
66 lb (30 kg)	2 lb 12¾ oz/1.27 kg
77 lb (35 kg)	2 lb 7¾ oz/1.13 kg

ENERGY

(per 3½ oz/100 g):	170 Cals

NUTRITIONAL BREAKDOWN   PAGE 130

METHOD

Boil the rice in plenty of water for at least 20 minutes (or 5 minutes longer than the cooking time indicated on the packet); it should be very soft.

Put the sliced carrots into a steamer or colander set over a pan of boiling water. Cover with a lid or tight-fitting foil. Steam for 5–8 minutes, until cooked, and let cool. Blend with a stick blender or food processor to a purée, and mix with the rice.

Sear the beef and spleen in a dry griddle pan, taking care not to brown (add a little water if necessary), for around 5 minutes. Let cool, blend to a creamy consistency, then mix in the oils and the supplement.

Put the meat into the dog bowl and serve the carrot risotto on top.

TIP

If you want to freeze this dish, boil the carrots with the rice, then dice the cooked meat and mix with the risotto, then freeze. Mix in the oils and dietary supplement at the last minute before serving.

TWIST

The spleen can be replaced with lung.

KEEP YOUR DOG'S HEALTH IN MIND

The spleen is a rich source of iron, which is an indispensable mineral during growth. At puppy stage, a dog's requirement for iron is about three times higher than that of an adult dog.

A NOTE ON SUPPLEMENTS

In this recipe the amount of Balance IT can be replaced with an equal amount of Complete Q.diet or Balance Trovet by increasing the amount of supplement 20% + ½ tablet of VMP Zoetis every 3 g of supplement.

Pasta with Carrot Sauce and Chicken

INGREDIENTS

2 LB 3¼ OZ/1 KG OF FOOD

Durum wheat semolina pasta	8 oz/225 g
Chicken breast or thigh, chopped	1¾ oz/50 g
Carrots, chopped	¾ cup/120 g
Chicken liver, chopped	4¼ oz/120 g
Salmon oil	1 tsp
Sunflower oil	1 ½ tbsp
Supplement (page 208)	3 tbsp + 1 tsp/24 g

WEIGHT OF ADULT: 6 LB 10 OZ/3 KG

WEIGHT OF PUPPY	MEAL SIZE
1 lb 15¾ oz (0.5 kg)	2⅞ oz/80 g
2 lb 3¼ oz (1 kg)	4¼ oz/120 g
4 lb 6 oz (2 kg)	6¼ oz/175 g

WEIGHT OF ADULT: 22 LB/10 KG

WEIGHT OF PUPPY	MEAL SIZE
6 lb 10 oz (3 kg)	9⅜ oz/265 g
13¼ lb (6 kg)	12⅞ oz/365 g
20 lb (9 kg)	14 oz/400 g

WEIGHT OF ADULT: 55 LB/25 KG

WEIGHT OF PUPPY	MEAL SIZE
11 lb (5 kg)	14¾ oz/420 g
22 lb (10 kg)	1 lb 4¾ oz/590 g
33 lb (15 kg)	1 lb 9¾ oz/730 g
44 lb (20 kg)	1 lb 9⅜ oz/720 g

WEIGHT OF ADULT: 88 LB/40 KG

WEIGHT OF PUPPY	MEAL SIZE
11 lb (5 kg)	14¾ oz/420 g
22 lb (10 kg)	1 lb 7 oz/650 g
33 lb (15 kg)	1 lb 12⅜ oz/805 g
44 lb (20 kg)	2 lb ½ oz/920 g
66 lb (30 kg)	2 lb 9⅜ oz/1.23 kg
77 lb (35 kg)	2 lb 6¾ oz/1.1 kg

ENERGY

(per 3½ oz/100 g):	179 Cals

NUTRITIONAL BREAKDOWN · PAGE 132

METHOD

Boil the pasta in plenty of water for at least 5 minutes more than the instructions given on the packet. It has to be very soft. Remember to rinse the pasta under running water if you cook it in advance, or if you want to refrigerate or freeze it.

Put the chopped chicken into a steamer or colander set over a pan of boiling water. Cover with a lid or tight-fitting foil and steam for 8–10 minutes, until cooked. Steam the carrots for 5–8 minutes. Let cool. Blend the carrots to a purée and combine with the pasta, diluting a little with the pasta cooking water. Chop the cooked chicken into very small pieces.

Sear the liver in a dry griddle pan, taking care not to brown it (add a little water if necessary.) It will take roughly 2 minutes to cook on each side. Leave it to cool, then chop it into very small pieces and mix it with the chicken.

Serve the pasta with the carrot sauce, and the chicken and liver on the side, mixed with the oils and dietary supplement.

TIP

If you're going to refrigerate or freeze this dish, remember to only add the oil and dietary supplement at the last minute before serving.

TWIST

Alternate the carrots with the same amount of zucchini (courgette), pumpkin, or half the amount of chicory.

KEEP YOUR DOG'S HEALTH IN MIND

Puppies have a high calcium requirement; however, be careful not to give too much, because an excess of calcium can be harmful, especially to larger breeds.

A NOTE ON SUPPLEMENTS

In this recipe the amount of Balance IT can be replaced with an equal amount of Complete Q.diet or even the same amount of Balance Trovet.

Meaty Rice Timbale with Pumpkin

INGREDIENTS

2 LB 3¼ OZ/1 KG OF FOOD

White rice	¾ oz/150 g
Pork neck or shoulder	12 oz/340 g
Pork spleen	6 ¾ oz/190 g
Pork heart	6 ¾ oz/190 g
Salmon oil	1 tsp
Flaxseed (linseed) oil	1 tbsp
Supplement (page 208)	3 tbsp/22 g
Pumpkin or other squash, diced	⅔ oz/90 g

WEIGHT OF ADULT: 6 LB 10 OZ/3 KG

WEIGHT OF PUPPY	MEAL SIZE
1 lb ⅝ oz (0.5 kg)	2⅝ oz/75 g
2 lb 3¼ oz (1 kg)	3⅞ oz/110 g
4 lb 6 oz (2 kg)	5⅝ oz/160 g

WEIGHT OF ADULT: 22 LB/10 KG

WEIGHT OF PUPPY	MEAL SIZE
6 lb 10 oz (3 kg)	9½ oz/270 g
13¼ lb (6 kg)	13⅜ oz/380 g
20 lb (9 kg)	14½ oz/410 g

WEIGHT OF ADULT: 55 LB/25 KG

WEIGHT OF PUPPY	MEAL SIZE
11 lb (5 kg)	15⅝ oz/445 g
22 lb (10 kg)	1 lb 5⅞ oz/620 g
33 lb (15 kg)	1 lb 11⅜ oz/775 g
44 lb (20 kg)	1 lb 10½ oz/750 g

WEIGHT OF ADULT: 88 LB/40 KG

WEIGHT OF PUPPY	MEAL SIZE
11 lb (5 kg)	15½ oz/440 g
22 lb (10 kg)	1 lb 8½ oz/695 g
33 lb (15 kg)	1 lb 14 oz/850 g
44 lb (20 kg)	2 lb 2⅜ oz/975 g
66 lb (30 kg)	2 lb 14 oz/1.3 kg
77 lb (35 kg)	2 lb 9¼ oz/1.17 kg

ENERGY

(per 3½ oz/100 g):	171 Cals

NUTRITIONAL BREAKDOWN   PAGE 134

METHOD

Boil the rice in plenty of water for at least 20 minutes (or 5 minutes longer than the cooking time indicated on the packet); it should be very soft. Drain and let cool.

Sear the pork, spleen, and heart in a dry griddle pan, taking care not to brown them (add a little water if necessary.) Each will take roughly 2 minutes to cook on both sides. Let cool, then cut into very small cubes and mix with the oil and the supplement.

Steam the diced pumpkin.

Arrange half of the rice in a ring, cover with the meat, followed by the pumpkin, then cover with the remaining rice.

TIP

You can boil the pumpkin with the rice, mix with the meat, and then freeze. Remember to only add any supplements, and the oil at the last minute before serving.

TWIST

If you are unable to find the pork offal, you can use the same weight of beef offal.

KEEP YOUR DOG'S HEALTH IN MIND

Using offal allows you to reduce the use of a dietary supplement because of its high nutrient content.

A NOTE ON SUPPLEMENTS

In this recipe the amount of Balance IT can be replaced with an equal amount of Complete Q.diet or an equal amount of Balance Trovet + ¼ tablet of VMP Zoetis for every 3 g of supplement.

ADULT
DOGS

Pasta with Soybeans and Crispy Apple

INGREDIENTS

2 LB 3¼ OZ/1 KG OF FOOD

Durum wheat semolina pasta	1¾ cups/130 g
Canned peas	4½ oz/130 g
Canned soybeans	¾ cup/315 g
Sunflower oil	2 tbsp, plus 7 tsp
Flaxseed (linseed) oil	5 tsp
Vegan supplement (page 208)	3⅜ oz/95 g
Supplement (page 208)	5 tbsp/38 g
Brewer's yeast or Marmite	2 tbsp
Apples, unpeeled, grated	1 cup/190 g

WEIGHT

DOG	MEAL SIZE
11 lb (5 kg)	5⅝ oz/160 g
22 lb (10 kg)	9½ oz/270 g
33 lb (15 kg)	12⅝ oz/360 g
44 lb (20 kg)	15⅝ oz/445 g
66 lb (30 kg)	1 lb/5⅜ oz/605 g
88 lb (40 kg)	1 lb 10⅜ oz/755 g

ENERGY

(per 3½ oz/100 g):	220 Cals

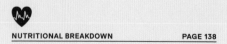

NUTRITIONAL BREAKDOWN   PAGE 138

METHOD

Boil the pasta in plenty of water for at least 5 minutes more than the instructions given on the packet. It has to be very soft.

Blend the peas and soybeans into a purée with a stick blender or in a food processor, combine with the pasta, and incorporate the oils, supplements, and yeast.

Serve the pasta in a bowl and top with the grated apples.

TIP

Remember to rinse the pasta under running water if you cook it in advance or if you want to refrigerate or freeze it. You can give your dog apple as a snack.

TWIST

Use fresh peas in spring instead of canned peas. As a general rule, if you don't plan to freeze the dish, use frozen legumes instead of canned because they don't contain added salt. For variation, swap the peas for the same weight of garbanzo beans (chickpeas).

KEEP YOUR DOG'S HEALTH IN MIND

Brewer's yeast is one of the best natural sources of vitamin B1, which helps keep your dog's claws and skin healthy, its coat shiny, and strengthens its immune and nervous systems.

ADULT DOGS

Vegetable and Cheese Rice Balls

INGREDIENTS

2 LB 3¼ OZ/1 KG OF FOOD

White rice	¾ cup, plus 2 tbsp/160 g
Canned peas	⅞ cup/155 g
Canned soybeans	⅞ cup/155 g
Sunflower oil	4 tsp
Supplement (page 208)	2¾ tbsp/21 g
Eggs	5 extra large/275 g
10% fat cottage cheese	⅞ cup/210 g

WEIGHT

DOG	MEAL SIZE
11 lb (5 kg)	6⅞ oz/195 g
22 lb (10 kg)	11¼ oz/320 g
33 lb (15 kg)	15½ oz/440 g
44 lb (20 kg)	1 lb 3 oz/540 g
66 lb (30 kg)	1 lb 10 oz/735 g
88 lb (40 kg)	2 lb ¼ oz/915 g

ENERGY

(per 3½ oz/100 g):	155 Cals

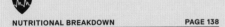

NUTRITIONAL BREAKDOWN   PAGE 138

METHOD

Boil the rice in plenty of water for at least 20 minutes, or 5 minutes longer than the cooking time indicated on the packet; it should be very soft. Drain, leaving it slightly damp. Press a little and let cool.

Blend the peas and soybeans into a purée with a stick blender or in a food processor, mix with the rice, oil, and dietary supplement, and shape into balls, using up completely.

Soft–boil the eggs, for a firm white and runny yolk, for around 6 minutes. Let cool and peel.

Serve the eggs on a bed of cottage cheese, with the rice balls on the side.

TIP

If you want to store the dish in the refrigerator for a few days together with the eggs, mix the cheese into the vegetables and rice. Otherwise, you can freeze the rice, cheese, and vegetables, but you have to soft–boil the eggs before serving.

TWIST

You can replace the peas with the same amount of lentils.

KEEP YOUR DOG'S HEALTH IN MIND

If your dog has had problems with uric acid stones, this dish is good for preventing them from re-forming.

Pasta with Soy Meatballs and Eggs

INGREDIENTS

2 LB 3¼ OZ/1 KG OF FOOD

Durum wheat semolina pasta	2½ cups/165 g
Canned soybeans	⅞ cup/435 g
Sheep ricotta cheese	1 cup/215 g
Eggs	3 large/145 g
Sunflower oil	2½ tsp
Supplement (page 208)	3⅔ tbsp/27 g

WEIGHT

DOG	MEAL SIZE
11 lb (5 kg)	6½ oz/185 g
22 lb (10 kg)	11 oz/310 g
33 lb (15 kg)	14¾ oz/420 g
44 lb (20 kg)	1 lb 2⅜ oz/520 g
66 lb (30 kg)	1 lb 8⅞ oz/705 g
88 lb (40 kg)	1 lb 14⅞ oz/875 g

ENERGY

(per 3½ oz/100 g):	164 Cals

NUTRITIONAL BREAKDOWN   PAGE 139

METHOD

Boil the pasta in plenty of water for at least 5 minutes more than the instructions given on the packet. It has to be very soft.

Blend the soybeans, mix with the cheese, and shape the mixture into balls.

Soft-boil the eggs to get firm whites and runny yolks, let cool, and peel. Don't worry if the recommended daily intake, based on the weight of your dog, is less than 1 egg; eggs can keep in the refrigerator for up to a week.

Mix the pasta with the oil and supplement. Add the meatballs and serve with the eggs on the side.

TIP

You could just mix the pasta with the cheese and soy balls and prepare the egg separately. This mix can then be stored in the refrigerator for several days.

TWIST

You can substitute double the amount of kefir for the sheep ricotta cheese.

KEEP YOUR DOG'S HEALTH IN MIND

If you prefer to use uncooked soybeans, remember to soak them in water for several hours, or better still, overnight, and cook them until they are very soft. If they aren't well cooked, they can be harmful to your dog's health.

Rice with Zucchini (Courgette)

INGREDIENTS

2 LB 3¼ OZ/1 KG OF FOOD

Brown rice	1 cup/175 g
Zucchini (courgette), sliced	2⅔ cups/305 g
Chicken breast or thigh, chopped	8¾ oz/250 g
Cod, chopped	8¾ oz/250 g
Corn oil	2½ tsp
Supplement (page 208)	2 tbsp/15 g

WEIGHT

DOG	MEAL SIZE
11 lb (5 kg)	9⅛ oz/260 g
22 lb (10 kg)	5½ oz/440 g
33 lb (15 kg)	1 lb 5⅛ oz/600 g
44 lb (20 kg)	1 lb 10 oz/740 g
66 lb (30 kg)	2 lb 3¾ oz/1 kg
88 lb (40 kg)	2¾ lb/1.25 kg

ENERGY

(per 3½ oz/100 g):	115 Cals

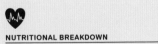

NUTRITIONAL BREAKDOWN   PAGE 139

METHOD

Boil the brown rice in plenty of water for at least 20 minutes (or at least 5 minutes longer than indicated on the packet): it should be very soft.

Boil the zucchini (courgette) for 5–8 minutes, or until cooked. Drain it and leave to cool, then blend with a stick blender or in a food processor until creamy in texture.

Put the chopped chicken and cod into a steamer or colander set over a pan of boiling water. Cover with a lid or tight-fitting foil and steam for 8–10 minutes, until cooked. Make sure there are no small bones in the fish. Leave to cool.

Combine the chicken and the fish with the brown rice, mix in the oil and add the supplement. Serve the risotto over the creamed zucchini (courgette).

TIP

If you're going to refrigerate or freeze it, boil the meat, fish, and zucchini (courgette) together, all cut into little pieces, then drain and add to the rice. Remember to add the oil and supplement only when you're about to serve it.

TWIST

Hake or plaice can be substituted for cod.

KEEP YOUR DOG'S HEALTH IN MIND

This recipe is suitable if your dog has had gastritis; there's much less than 15% fat, so it won't irritate your pet's stomach.

Layered Rice, Fish, and Vegetables

INGREDIENTS

2 LB 3¼ OZ/1 KG OF FOOD

White rice	⅞ cup/165 g
Hake, skinless, chopped	1 lb 4⅝ oz/585 g
Green beans	1⅔ cups/185 g
Corn oil	3 tbsp
Supplement (page 208)	2½ tbsp/19 g

WEIGHT

DOG	MEAL SIZE
11 lb (5 kg)	7½ oz/215 g
22 lb (10 kg)	12⅝ oz/360 g
33 lb (15 kg)	1 lb 1¼ oz/490 g
44 lb (20 kg)	1 lb 5½ oz/610 g
66 lb (30 kg)	1 lb 13 oz/825 g
88 lb (40 kg)	2 lb 3¼ oz/1 kg

ENERGY

(per 3½ oz/100 g):	141 Cals

NUTRITIONAL BREAKDOWN   PAGE 140

METHOD

Boil the rice in plenty of water for at least 20 minutes, or at least 5 minutes longer than indicated on the packet; it should be very soft. Drain and leave to cool.

Put the hake into a steamer or colander set over a pan of boiling water. Cover with a lid or tight-fitting foil and steam for 8–10 minutes, until cooked. Make sure there are no bones in the fish.

Boil the green beans, drain, and leave to cool.

Use the green beans for the first layer, the rice for the second, then top with a layer of hake. Drizzle with the oil and add the supplement.

TIP

The green beans can also be cut up and boiled with the rice, to which the cooked hake can then be added, either blended or flaked. This can then be frozen. In this case, remember to mix with the oil and add the supplement just before serving.

KEEP YOUR DOG'S HEALTH IN MIND

If your dog is losing weight, substitute the white rice for brown rice. In cases of gastritis, this is the perfect recipe to get your pet back on its feet.

Puffed Rice Patties

INGREDIENTS

2 LB 3¼ OZ/1 KG OF FOOD

Puffed rice	13½ oz/190 g
Lean veal, chopped	11⅛ oz/315 g
Fresh whole sardines	6¾ oz/190 g
Green beans	2 cups/220 g
Supplement (page 208)	3⅓ tbsp/25 g
Sunflower oil	4½ tbsp

WEIGHT

DOG	MEAL SIZE
11 lb (5 kg)	5⅝ oz/160 g
22 lb (10 kg)	9½ oz/270 g
33 lb (15 kg)	12⅝ oz/360 g
44 lb (20 kg)	1 lb/450 g
66 lb (30 kg)	1 lb 5½ oz/610 g
88 lb (40 kg)	1 lb 10¾ oz/760 g

ENERGY

(per 3½ oz/100 g):	190 Cals

NUTRITIONAL BREAKDOWN — PAGE 140

METHOD

Soak the puffed rice in water for 10–15 minutes. Meanwhile, put the veal into a steamer or colander set over a pan of boiling water. Cover with a lid or tight-fitting foil and steam for 8–10 minutes, until cooked. Let cool and chop finely.

Sear the sardines on a griddle using no fat or oil, taking care not to brown them, around 2 minutes on each side. Leave to cool and chop finely—this way, the bones will not be a problem for your dog.

Boil the beans, drain, and leave to cool. Drain the puffed rice.

Combine the puffed rice with the veal and sardines, add the supplement and shape into small balls. Flatten, with the palms of your hands, into patties, and serve with the green beans mixed with the oil.

TIP

If you'd like to make just one mixture and reduce the prep time, cook the green beans with the veal, then chop both finely and combine with the sardines and the rice. Mix with the oil and add the supplement just before serving the food.

TWIST

Fresh anchovies can be substituted for the sardines.

KEEP YOUR DOG'S HEALTH IN MIND

Oily fish is an important source of omega-3 polyunsaturated fatty acids.

Cod and Potato Casserole

INGREDIENTS

2 LB 3¼ OZ/1 KG OF FOOD

Cod, cut into small pieces	1 lb 2 oz/510 g
White skinless potatoes, diced	3 cups/440 g
Sunflower oil	2½ tbsp
Supplement (page 208)	2 tbsp/14 g

WEIGHT

DOG	MEAL SIZE
11 lb (5 kg)	10⅜ oz/295 g
22 lb (10 kg)	1 lb 1½ oz/495 g
33 lb (15 kg)	1 lb 7⅝ oz/670 g
44 lb (20 kg)	1 lb 13¼ oz/830 g
66 lb (30 kg)	2 lb 6¾ oz/1.1 kg
88 lb (40 kg)	3 lb 1⅜ oz/1.4 kg

ENERGY

(per 3½ oz/100 g):	103 Cals

NUTRITIONAL BREAKDOWN PAGE 141

METHOD

Put the cod into a steamer or colander set over a pan of boiling water. Cover with a lid or tight-fitting foil and steam for 8–10 minutes, until cooked. Let cool and chop finely.

Boil the potatoes in plenty of water. Drain and let cool, then mash well with a fork.

Mix the fish with the mashed potato. Incorporate the oil and supplement and serve.

TIP

It's always better to prepare meals containing potatoes fresh on the day, so that there is no need for freezing.

TWIST

You can replace the potatoes with the same weight of sweet potatoes.

KEEP YOUR DOG'S HEALTH IN MIND

This recipe is perfect for an elimination diet for diagnosing any adverse reactions to food.

ADULT DOGS

Turkey and Rice Meatballs

INGREDIENTS

2 LB 3¼ OZ/1 KG OF FOOD

White rice	1¼ cups/220 g
Skinless turkey breast, chopped	15⅝ oz/445 g
Carrots, chopped	1 cup/110 g
Zucchini (courgette), sliced	1¼ cups/140 g
Sunflower oil	2 tbsp
Berries (blueberries, goji berries)	¼ cup/30 g
Supplement (page 208)	3 tbsp/22 g

WEIGHT

DOG	MEAL SIZE
11 lb (5 kg)	6⅜ oz/180 g
22 lb (10 kg)	10½ oz/300 g
33 lb (15 kg)	14½ oz/410 g
44 lb (20 kg)	1 lb 2 oz/510 g
66 lb (30 kg)	1 lb 8⅜ oz/690 g
88 lb (40 kg)	1 lb 14⅜ oz/860 g

ENERGY

(per 3½ oz/100 g):	168 Cals

NUTRITIONAL BREAKDOWN   PAGE 141

METHOD

Boil the rice in plenty of water for at least 20 minutes (or at least 5 minutes longer than indicated on the packet): it should be very soft. Drain it but keep it slightly moist, then mash and leave to cool.

Put the turkey and carrots into a steamer or colander set over a pan of boiling water. Cover with a lid or tight-fitting foil and steam for 8–10 minutes, until cooked. Let cool and chop finely.

Boil the zucchini (courgette) for 5–8 minutes, then drain. Leave to cool.

Mix the rice, meat, and carrots with the oil, add the berries and the supplement, and shape into balls. Serve the meatballs with the zucchini (courgette).

TIP

If you'd like to prepare this in advance and freeze it, cook the zucchini (courgette) with the carrots and the meat, and add to the meatballs.

TWIST

To change the flavor of the food, replace half the weight of the turkey with twice the amount of cod.

KEEP YOUR DOG'S HEALTH IN MIND

When your dog is molting, substitute half the amount of sunflower oil with flaxseed (linseed) oil: it's high in omega-3 and omega-6 and helps to make their coat shinier.

Turkey and Ricotta Quenelles

INGREDIENTS

2 LB 3¼ OZ/1 KG OF FOOD

Puffed rice	12 cups/170 g
Skinless turkey breast, chopped	11¾ oz/335 g
Ricotta cheese	⅞ cup/225 g
Sunflower oil	1½ tbsp
Supplement (page 208)	3 tbsp/22 g
Carrots, grated	2 cups/225 g

WEIGHT

DOG	MEAL SIZE
11 lb (5 kg)	6⅜ oz/180 g
22 lb (10 kg)	10½ oz/300 g
33 lb (15 kg)	14 oz/400 g
44 lb (20 kg)	1 lb 1⅝ oz/500 g
66 lb (30 kg)	1½ lb/680 g
88 lb (40 kg)	1 lb 13¾ oz/845 g

ENERGY

(per 3½ oz/100 g):	163 Cals

NUTRITIONAL BREAKDOWN   PAGE 142

METHOD

Soak the puffed rice in water for 10–15 minutes. Meanwhile, put the turkey into a steamer or colander set over a pan of boiling water. Cover with a lid or tight-fitting foil and steam for 8–10 minutes, until cooked. Let cool and chop finely.

Mix the turkey into the ricotta. Add the puffed rice, sunflower oil, and supplement. Shape into quenelles, or oval–shaped meatballs.

Serve the quenelles on a bed of grated carrots.

TIP

If you'd like to prepare this in advance and freeze it, steam the carrots (cut into rounds) together with the turkey and mash with a fork. Finely chop the meat and ricotta, and add both to the puffed rice. In this case, remember to mix with the oil and add the supplement just before serving.

TWIST

If your dog likes low-fat plain yogurt, substitute it for half of the ricotta: this meal will then be a little lighter.

KEEP YOUR DOG'S HEALTH IN MIND

If you substitute all the ricotta for yogurt, the amount of fat will be reduced by 9% and the recipe will be good for a dog that's less physically active.

Oats, Turkey, and Potatoes

INGREDIENTS

2 LB 3¼ OZ/1 KG OF FOOD

Oat flakes	2⅓ cups/120 g
Skinless turkey breast	15½ oz/440 g
Potatoes, peeled and diced	1⅔ cups/245 g
Kefir	⅔ cup/145 ml
Sunflower oil	5 tsp
Supplement (page 208)	3⅓ tbsp/24 g

WEIGHT

DOG	MEAL SIZE
11 lb (5 kg)	7¼ oz/205 g
22 lb (10 kg)	12⅛ oz/345 g
33 lb (15 kg)	1 lb ⅜ oz/465 g
44 lb (20 kg)	1 lb 4½ oz/580 g
66 lb (30 kg)	1 lb 11⅝ oz/785 g
88 lb (40 kg)	2 lb 2⅜ oz/975 g

ENERGY

(per 3½ oz/100 g):	147 Cals

NUTRITIONAL BREAKDOWN   PAGE 142

METHOD

Boil the oat flakes in plenty of water and cook for at least 5 minutes longer than is indicated on the packet: they should be very soft. Drain, but not entirely, as the mix should be like porridge. Leave to cool.

Sear the turkey on a griddle using no fat or oil, taking care not to brown it (if necessary, use a little water to prevent this). Leave to cool. Shred the meat and chop finely, then add to the oats.

Put the potatoes into a steamer or colander set over a pan of boiling water. Cover with a lid or tight–fitting foil and steam for 10 minutes, until cooked. Leave to cool, then mash with the kefir.

Mix the oats and turkey with the oil and add the supplement. Serve with the potatoes mashed with the kefir.

TIP

If you steam the turkey (cut into little pieces) with the potatoes, you can then finely chop everything, add it to the oats, then freeze. When it's thawed, mix in the kefir, oil and add the supplement.

TWIST

If you like, the oat flakes can be substituted with barley flakes.

KEEP YOUR DOG'S HEALTH IN MIND

Sneak cereal flakes (spelt, oats, or millet) into your dog's food as they provide insoluble fiber that's helpful if your pet is constipated.

Cornmeal with Cheddar and Chicken

INGREDIENTS

2 LB 3¼ OZ/1 KG OF FOOD

Chicken breast or thigh, chopped	7 oz/200 g
Squash, finely diced	1 cup/205 g
Chicken livers, cleaned	4¾ oz/135 g
Cornmeal (instant polenta)	1⅛ cups/200 g
Cheddar cheese, grated	2⅓ cups/200 g
Sunflower oil	3 tbsp
Supplement (page 208)	3⅔ tbsp/34 g

WEIGHT

DOG	MEAL SIZE
11 lb (5 kg)	5¼ oz/150 g
22 lb (10 kg)	8¾ oz/250 g
33 lb (15 kg)	12 oz/340 g
44 lb (20 kg)	14¾ oz/420 g
66 lb (30 kg)	1¼ lb/570 g
88 lb (40 kg)	1 lb 9 oz/710 g

ENERGY

(per 3½ oz/100 g):	203 Cals

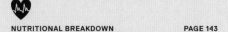

NUTRITIONAL BREAKDOWN	PAGE 143

METHOD

Put the chicken and squash into a steamer or colander set over a pan of boiling water. Cover with a lid or tight–fitting foil and steam for 8–10 minutes, until cooked. Let cool and chop finely.

Sear the chicken livers on a griddle using no fat or oil, taking care not to brown them. If necessary, use a little water to prevent this; it will take around 2 minutes on each side. Leave to cool, chop finely, and add to the chicken and squash.

Make the instant polenta by boiling the cornmeal in water for at least 5 minutes longer than indicated on the packet. When it's done, add the grated cheese and leave to cool.

Mix the chicken and vegetables with the oil and the supplement and serve with the cornmeal (instant polenta).

TWIST

Substitute the chicken for the same amount of quail.

KEEP YOUR DOG'S HEALTH IN MIND

Alternate the chicken livers with the same amount of eggs: the meal will be higher in essential amino acids, the most important nutrients for maintaining muscular mass.

Roman-Style Stuffed Rice Balls

INGREDIENTS

2 LB 3¼ OZ/1 KG OF FOOD

White rice	¾ cup/140 g
Chicken breast, chopped	12⅞ oz/365 g
Sunflower oil	3½ tsp
Flaxseed (linseed) oil	3½ tsp
Salmon oil	3½ tsp
Parmesan cheese, grated	¾ cup/90 g
Maltodextrin	¼ cup/46 g
Supplement (page 208)	3¾ tbsp/28 g
Apples, unpeeled, grated	1¾ cups/275 g

WEIGHT

DOG	MEAL SIZE
11 lb (5 kg)	8⅛ oz/220 g
22 lb (10 kg)	12⅞ oz/365 g
33 lb (15 kg)	1 lb 1⅝ oz/500 g
44 lb (20 kg)	1 lb 5⅞ oz/620 g
66 lb (30 kg)	1 lb 13½ oz/835 g
88 lb (40 kg)	2 lb 5 oz/1.05 kg

ENERGY

(per 3½ oz/100 g):	229 Cals

NUTRITIONAL BREAKDOWN PAGE 143

METHOD

Boil the rice in plenty of water for at least 20 minutes (or 5 minutes longer than the cooking time indicated); it should be very soft. Drain and leave to cool.

Put the chicken into a steamer or colander set over a pan of boiling water. Cover with a lid or tight-fitting foil and steam for 8–10 minutes, until cooked. Let cool and chop finely.

Mix the rice with the oils and cheese. Incorporate the maltodextrin and supplement into the chicken.

Take one heaped tbsp of rice and spread it out over the work surface. Arrange a few chicken pieces over it and cover with another tbsp of rice.

Keeping the rice over the filling, shape into large, oblong–shaped meatballs, and serve sprinkled with grated apple.

TIP

If you're in a hurry, you can cook the chicken pieces with the rice, then mix all of the ingredients together, including the grated apple. This is great for freezing.

TWIST

The chicken can be replaced with the same amount of rabbit.

KEEP YOUR DOG'S HEALTH IN MIND

Maltodextrin is an easily absorbed, meaning this is a good before a long walk.

ADULT DOGS

Chicken and Apple Meatballs

INGREDIENTS

2 LB 3¼ OZ/1 KG OF FOOD

White rice	⅞ cup/160 g
Chicken breast, chopped	1 lb ¼ oz/460 g
Pumpkin, diced	½ cup/125 g
Apples, unpeeled, grated	1 cup/125 g
Salmon oil	1 tbsp
Supplement (page 208)	3½ tbsp/26 g
Pork fat (lard)	1 tbsp/14 g
Sunflower oil	2 tbsp
Flaxseed (linseed) oil	1 tbsp
Parmesan cheese, grated	⅓ cup/35 g

WEIGHT

DOG	MEAL SIZE
11 lb (5 kg)	5½ oz/155 g
22 lb (10 kg)	9 oz/260 g
33 lb (15 kg)	1¼ oz/350 g
44 lb (20 kg)	1 lb/440 g
66 lb (30 kg)	1 lb 3 oz/595 g
88 lb (40 kg)	1 lb 6 oz/750 g

ENERGY

(per 3½ oz/100 g):	194 Cals

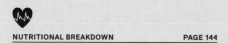

NUTRITIONAL BREAKDOWN   PAGE 144

METHOD

Boil the rice in plenty of water for at least 20 minutes, or 5 minutes longer than the cooking time indicated on the packet; it should be very soft. Let cool.

Put the chicken and pumpkin into a steamer or colander set over a pan of boiling water. Cover with a lid or tight-fitting foil and steam for 8–10 minutes, until cooked. Let cool and chop finely.

Mix the grated apple with the chicken, then add the salmon oil, supplement, and pork fat. Shape into meatballs.

Mix the pumpkin with the rice, season with the sunflower and flaxseed (linseed) oil and the grated cheese, and serve with the meatballs.

TIP

If you're in a hurry, you can boil the rice together with the chicken and pumpkin. Combine with the grated apple and cheese before shaping into meatballs. Mix in the oils, fat, and dietary supplement at the last minute before serving.

TWIST

You can also make this dish without the apples, and save them for a snack.

KEEP YOUR DOG'S HEALTH IN MIND

Unpeeled apples are a source of soluble fiber, important for gut microbiota.

ADULT DOGS

ADULT DOGS

Soft-Boiled Egg with Squash and Chicken

INGREDIENTS

2 LB 3¼ OZ/1 KG OF FOOD

White rice	1⅓ cups/255 g
Squash, finely chopped	1⅓ cups/195 g
Chicken breast or thigh	13⅜ oz/380 g
Egg	1 large/95 g
Sunflower oil	2 tbsp
Salmon oil	1½ tsp
Supplement (page 208)	3 ⅓ tbsp/25 g

WEIGHT

DOG	MEAL SIZE
11 lb (5 kg)	5½ oz/155 g
22 lb (10 kg)	9⅛ oz/260 g
33 lb (15 kg)	12⅝ oz/360 g
44 lb (20 kg)	15⅝ oz/445 g
66 lb (30 kg)	1 lb 5⅛ oz/600 g
88 lb (40 kg)	1 lb 10½ oz/750 g

ENERGY

(per 3½ oz/100 g):	192 Cals

NUTRITIONAL BREAKDOWN	PAGE 144

METHOD

Boil the rice and the squash in plenty of water, for at least 20 minutes (and at least 5 minutes longer than is indicated on the rice packet): the rice should be very soft. Drain the rice and squash and leave to cool.

Sear the chicken on a griddle using no fat or oil, taking care not to brown it; if necessary, use a little water to prevent this. It should take around 8 minutes. Leave to cool and chop finely.

Soft-boil the egg so that the white is cooked and the yolk is runny, around 6 minutes. Leave it to cool, then peel and chop.

Combine the chicken with the rice and squash, then add the sunflower and salmon oils, then the supplement. Place the soft-boiled egg on top and serve.

TIP

The mixture will keep in the refrigerator for a few days, as will the egg. You can also freeze the rice, chicken, and squash, and soft-boil the egg before serving.

TWIST

If your dog enjoys different flavors, you can substitute the egg with 1¾ oz (50 g) of fish or 1⅜ oz (40 g) of beef liver.

KEEP YOUR DOG'S HEALTH IN MIND

Salmon oil contains important fatty acids such as EPA (eicosapentaenoic), which has an anti-inflammatory effect on joints.

Chicken, Pork, and Vegetable Rice

INGREDIENTS

2 LB 3¼ OZ/1 KG OF FOOD

White rice	½ cup/95 g
Green beans, finely chopped	1⅓ cups/145 g
Carrots, sliced	1¼ cups/145 g
Sunflower oil	1 tbsp
Pork neck or shoulder	15½ oz/440 g
Chicken giblets	5⅛ oz/145 g
Supplement (page 208)	2 tbsp/14 g

WEIGHT

DOG	MEAL SIZE
11 lb (5 kg)	7⅜ oz/210 g
22 lb (10 kg)	12⅜ oz/350 g
33 lb (15 kg)	1 lb ¾ oz/475 g
44 lb (20 kg)	1 lb 4½ oz/580 g
66 lb (30 kg)	1¾ lb/790 g
88 lb (40 kg)	2 lb 2 oz/990 g

ENERGY

(per 3½ oz/100 g):	145 Cals

NUTRITIONAL BREAKDOWN   PAGE 145

METHOD

Boil the rice in plenty of water for at least 20 minutes (or for at least 5 minutes longer than is indicated on the packet): it should be very soft. Drain, then mash and leave to cool.

Put the vegetables into a steamer or colander set over boiling water. Cover with a lid or tight-fitting foil and steam for 5–8 minutes, until cooked. Let cool.

Sear the pork and the giblets on a griddle using no fat or oil, taking care not to brown them; if necessary, use a little water to prevent this. It will take around 5–8 minutes. Leave to cool, chop finely, combine with the rice, and add the supplement.

Shape the rice and meat into a large meatloaf; cut into slices and serve with the vegetables, mixed with the oil.

TIP

After cooking the vegetables, you could also finely chop and combine with the rice and meat, then freeze. You'll need to add the oil and supplement just before serving.

TWIST

Substitute the chicken giblets for fresh cod, adding 20 percent more fish than you would have done of meat, if you like.

KEEP YOUR DOG'S HEALTH IN MIND

High protein helps to increase lean mass and activate metabolism; good if your dog is overweight.

Duck and Quinoa Salad

INGREDIENTS

2 LB 3¼ OZ/1 KG OF FOOD

Quinoa	1½ cups/250 g
Duck breast, skin on	11 oz/310 g
Zucchini (courgette)	1 medium/185 g
Carrots (prepared)	1⅓ cups/185 g
Flaxseed (linseed) oil	5 tsp
Sunflower oil	5 tsp
Extra virgin olive oil	5 tsp
Supplement (page 208)	4 tbsp/31 g

WEIGHT

DOG	MEAL SIZE
11 lb (5 kg)	5⅝ oz/160 g
22 lb (10 kg)	9⅜ oz/265 g
33 lb (15 kg)	13 oz/370 g
44 lb (20 kg)	1 lb ¼ oz/460 g
66 lb (30 kg)	1 lb 5⅞ oz/620 g
88 lb (40 kg)	1 lb 11 oz/775 g

ENERGY

(per 3½ oz/100 g):	183 Cals

NUTRITIONAL BREAKDOWN   PAGE 145

METHOD

Boil the quinoa in plenty of water for 5 minutes longer than the time indicated on the packet; it should be very soft.

In the meantime, cook the duck on a very hot, dry griddle pan, browning the surface while leaving the inside soft. It should take around 8 minutes. Remove the skin and cut the flesh into thin strips.

Wash, peel, and cut the carrots and zucchini (courgette) into julienne strips.

Mix all of the ingredients together then mix with the oils and supplement before serving.

TWIST

You can swap the quinoa for white potatoes, tripling the weight. Also, if your dog doesn't like raw vegetables, steam and finely chop them, then mix them with the quinoa.

KEEP YOUR DOG'S HEALTH IN MIND

Quinoa is a pseudocereal that contains proteins which are particularly suitable for dogs who show adverse reactions to the protein in cereals.

Rabbit Stew with Potatoes and Kefir

INGREDIENTS

2 LB 3¼ OZ/1 KG OF FOOD

Rabbit thigh	14¼ oz/405 g
White potatoes, diced	2¾ cups/405 g
Kefir	⅔ cup/145 ml
Corn oil	2 tbsp
Supplement (page 208)	2 tbsp/15 g

WEIGHT

DOG	MEAL SIZE
11 lb (5 kg)	9½ oz/270 g
22 lb (10 kg)	1 lb/455 g
33 lb (15 kg)	1 lb 5⅞ oz/620 g
44 lb (20 kg)	1 lb 11⅛ oz/770 g
66 lb (30 kg)	2 lb 4⅘ oz/1.13 kg
88 lb (40 kg)	2 lb 14 oz/1.3 kg

ENERGY

(per 3½ oz/100 g):	111 Cals

NUTRITIONAL BREAKDOWN　　　　PAGE 146

METHOD

Sear the rabbit in a dry griddle pan, taking care not to brown. Add a little water if necessary; this will take around 5–8 minutes. Let cool, then cut into bite-sized pieces.

Put the potatoes into a steamer or colander set over a pan of boiling water. Cover with a lid or tight-fitting foil and steam for 8–10 minutes, until cooked. Let cool. Combine with the rabbit and kefir.

Mix in the oil and supplement before serving.

TIP

You can prepare the rabbit in advance and mix with the kefir before freezing. Cook the rest to serve.

TWIST

You can replace the kefir with cow's milk ricotta, halving the weight.

KEEP YOUR DOG'S HEALTH IN MIND

The potatoes should be cooked fresh rather than being cooked and stored in the refrigerator. Carbohydrates can form resistant starch, a process that commonly occurs with potatoes, making them less digestible for your pet.

Corn Pasta with Rabbit

INGREDIENTS

2 LB 3¼ OZ/1 KG OF FOOD

Corn pasta	6⅜ oz/180 g
Squash, peeled and diced	1¾ cups/210 g
Zucchini (courgette), diced	1⅔ cups/210 g
Rabbit thigh	12 oz/340 g
Corn oil	2 tbsp, plus 2 tsp
Supplement (page 208)	2¾ tbsp/21 g

WEIGHT

DOG	MEAL SIZE
11 lb (5 kg)	6⅞ oz/195 g
22 lb (10 kg)	11¼ oz/320 g
33 lb (15 kg)	15⅜ oz/435 g
44 lb (20 kg)	1 lb 3⅜ oz/550 g
66 lb (30 kg)	1 lb 10 oz/740 g
88 lb (40 kg)	2 lb/910 g

ENERGY

ENERGY (per 3½ oz/100 g):	159 Cals

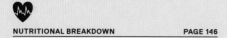

NUTRITIONAL BREAKDOWN   PAGE 146

METHOD

Boil the pasta in plenty of water and cook for at least 5 minutes longer than indicated on the packet: it should be very soft.

Put the squash and zucchini (courgette) into a steamer or colander set over a pan of boiling water. Cover with a lid or tight-fitting foil and steam for 8–10 minutes, until cooked. Let cool and mash well with a fork.

Sear the rabbit on a griddle using no fat or oil, taking care not to brown it. If necessary, use a little water to prevent this; it should take around 8–10 minutes. Leave to cool, then finely chop.

Serve the pasta over the vegetable mash and top with the rabbit. Mix with the oil and add the supplement.

TIP

The rabbit, chopped finely, can also be boiled with the squash and zucchini (courgette).

TWIST

You can substitute part of the corn pasta with an equal amount of cornflakes; make sure they don't contain sugar.

KEEP YOUR DOG'S HEALTH IN MIND

Corn oil is an excellent source of essential fatty acids, to keep your dog's coat healthy.

Pork with Green Beans

INGREDIENTS

2 LB 3¼ OZ/1 KG OF FOOD

Durum wheat semolina pasta	8 oz/225 g
Pork neck or shoulder	1 lb 2 oz/510 g
Dried rosemary	1 tsp
Lard or suet	1 tbsp/17 g
Green beans	1¾ cups/200 g
Sunflower oil	1 tbsp
Supplement (page 208)	3 tbsp/23 g

WEIGHT

DOG	MEAL SIZE
11 lb (5 kg)	6¼ oz/175 g
22 lb (10 kg)	10⅜ oz/295 g
33 lb (15 kg)	14 oz/400 g
44 lb (20 kg)	1 lb 1⅝ oz/500 g
66 lb (30 kg)	1 lb 7⅝ oz/670 g
88 lb (40 kg)	1 lb 13⅝ oz/840 g

ENERGY

(per 3½ oz/100 g):	171 Cals

NUTRITIONAL BREAKDOWN   PAGE 147

METHOD

Boil the pasta in plenty of water and cook for at least 5 minutes longer than indicated on the packet: it should be very soft.

Sear the pork on a griddle using no fat or oil, taking care not to brown it. If necessary, use a little water to prevent this; it should take around 8–10 minutes. Leave the meat to cool then finely chop. Add the rosemary and the lard or suet.

Put the green beans into a steamer or colander set over a pan of boiling water. Cover with a lid or tight-fitting foil and steam for 5–8 minutes, until cooked. When cool, chop the beans.

Combine the pasta with the pork. Serve alongside the beans, adding the oil and supplement before serving.

TIP

If you prefer, cut the beans into small pieces and add them to the pasta and the pork. This will make it more convenient to freeze and use when needed. Mix with the oil and the supplement only when you're about to serve it.

TWIST

Eggs are a very good source of protein; reduce the meat by 1¾ oz (50 g) twice a week and add a soft-boiled egg.

KEEP YOUR DOG'S HEALTH IN MIND

Pork is one of the best sources of meat with omega-6/omega-3.

Pasta Salad with Pork, Endives, and Yogurt

INGREDIENTS

2 LB 3¼ OZ/1 KG OF FOOD

Semolina pasta	7 oz/200 g
Pork neck or shoulder	14 oz/400 g
Whole (full-fat) milk yogurt	6 tbsp/175 ml
Supplement (page 208)	3 tbsp/23 g
Endives	2 heads/170 g
Sunflower oil	2¾ tbsp

WEIGHT

DOG	MEAL SIZE
11 lb (5 kg)	6¼ oz/175 g
22 lb (10 kg)	10⅜ oz/295 g
33 lb (15 kg)	14 oz/400 g
44 lb (20 kg)	1 lb 1⅝ oz/500 g
66 lb (30 kg)	1 lb 7⅝ oz/670 g
88 lb (40 kg)	1 lb 13¼ oz/830 g

ENERGY

(per 3½ oz/100 g):	168 Cals

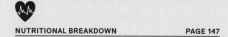

NUTRITIONAL BREAKDOWN PAGE 147

METHOD

Boil the pasta in plenty of water and cook at least 5 minutes longer than indicated on the packet: it should be very soft.

Sear the pork on a griddle using no fat or oil, taking care not to brown it. If necessary, use a little water to prevent this; it should take around 8–10 minutes. Leave to cool, finely chop and add the yogurt and the supplement.

Boil the endives in plenty of water until cooked, around 4–5 minutes. Drain, squeeze out the excess water and cut them up. Add them to the pasta, mix with the oil, and leave to cool.

Combine the pasta and meat, mix well then serve.

TIP

Remember to wash the pasta under running water if you're cooking it in advance or if you're going to refrigerate or freeze the food.

TWIST

If you like, you can substitute corn oil for the sunflower oil; your dog's fatty acid requirements will still be met.

KEEP YOUR DOG'S HEALTH IN MIND

If you substitute the sunflower oil for the same amount of salmon or krill oil this will make the meal higher in EPA, a fatty acid which is an excellent means of keeping your dog's coat shiny and its skin healthy and well hydrated.

Cornmeal with Surf and Turf

INGREDIENTS

2 LB 3¼ OZ/1 KG OF FOOD

Chicken breast, finely chopped	8¾ oz/250 g
Hake, finely chopped	14 oz/400 g
Green beans	1 cup/100 g
Cornmeal (instant polenta)	1⅛ cups/200 g
Sunflower oil	4 tsp
Psyllium husks	3 tbsp
Supplement (page 208)	4 tsp/20 g

WEIGHT

DOG	MEAL SIZE
11 lb (5 kg)	7 oz/200 g
22 lb (10 kg)	11¾ oz/335 g
33 lb (15 kg)	2⅔ cups/460 g
44 lb (20 kg)	1 lb 3⅞ oz/565 g
66 lb (30 kg)	1 lb 11 oz/765 g
88 lb (40 kg)	2 lb 1⅝ oz/955 g

ENERGY

(per 3½ oz/100 g):	147 Cals

NUTRITIONAL BREAKDOWN   PAGE 148

METHOD

Put the chicken and hake into a steamer or colander set over a pan of boiling water. Cover with a lid or tight-fitting foil and steam for 8–10 minutes, until cooked. Once cool, finely chop.

Boil the green beans in plenty of water until cooked, around 4–5 minutes, and leave to cool.

Make the cornmeal (instant polenta) by boiling it in water for at least 5 minutes longer than is indicated on the packet. Leave to cool.

Mix the chicken and fish with the sunflower oil, add the psyllium husks, and serve the stew with the cornmeal (instant polenta) and green beans.

TIP

If you like, chop the green beans and steam them together with the meat and fish, then mix with the cornmeal (instant polenta) and freeze.

TWIST

You can use carrots instead of green beans if you increase the amount by 20%.

KEEP YOUR DOG'S HEALTH IN MIND

Psyllium husks are the outer parts of the seeds of the plantago plant and are an excellent source of soluble fiber for your pet's diet.

Surf and Turf Rice and Potato Ring

INGREDIENTS

2 LB 3¼ OZ/1 KG OF FOOD

White rice	¾ cup/155 g
White potatoes, chopped	1¾ cups/260 g
Cod, diced	7⅜ oz/210 g
Lean veal, diced	11⅛ oz/315 g
Lard	1 tbsp/21 g
Supplement (page 208)	2¾ tbsp/21 g
Corn oil	4 tsp

WEIGHT

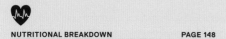

DOG	MEAL SIZE
11 lb (5 kg)	6¾ oz/190 g
22 lb (10 kg)	11¼ oz/320 g
33 lb (15 kg)	15½ oz/440 g
44 lb (20 kg)	1 lb 3 oz/540 g
66 lb (30 kg)	1 lb 10 oz/735 g
88 lb (40 kg)	2 lb ½ oz/920 g

ENERGY

(per 3½ oz/100 g):	161 Cals

NUTRITIONAL BREAKDOWN   PAGE 148

METHOD

Boil the rice together with the potatoes in plenty of water for at least 20 minutes or at least 5 minutes longer than indicated on the rice packet; both ingredients should be very soft. Drain, leave to cool, and mash the potatoes.

Put the cod and veal into a steamer or colander set over a pan of boiling water. Cover with a lid or tight-fitting foil and steam for 8–10 minutes, until cooked. Once cool, finely chop.

Add the lard and the supplement to the rice and potatoes, and add the oil to the meat and fish. Shape the rice and potatoes into a ring and fill it with the cod and veal.

TIP

If you wish to prepare this in advance and freeze it, boil all the ingredients together and then mix well; mix with the oil and add the supplement just before serving.

TWIST

If your dog is more physically active, substitute the veal for beef.

KEEP YOUR DOG'S HEALTH IN MIND

For a dog, lard is an excellent source of energy as they rarely suffer from high cholesterol; besides, high cholesterol is not linked to the presence of animal fats in dogs' diets.

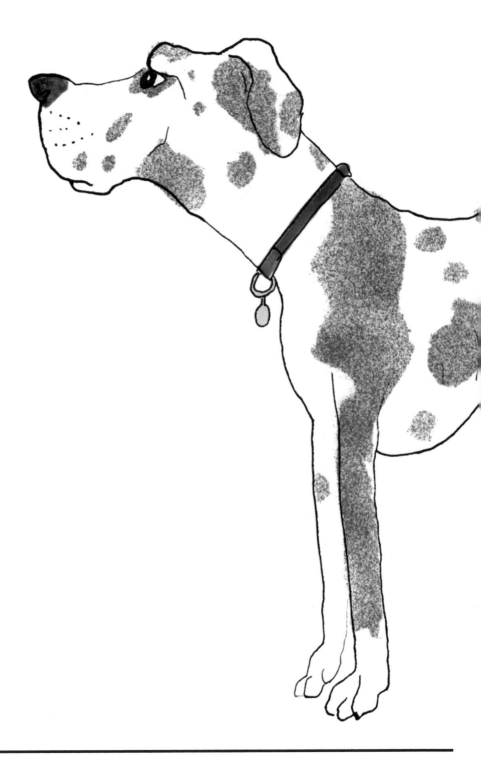

ADULT DOGS

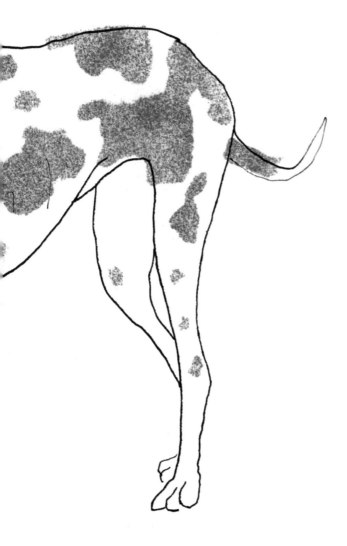

ADULT DOGS

Pasta with Zucchini (Courgette) and Lamb

INGREDIENTS

2 LB 3¼ OZ/1 KG OF FOOD

Durum wheat semolina pasta	7¾ oz/220 g
Zucchini (courgette), sliced	2 cups/220 g
Lean lamb, chopped	13¾ oz/390 g
Beef heart	5 oz/140 g
Sunflower oil	⅛ tsp
Supplement (page 208)	3 tbsp/22 g

WEIGHT

DOG	MEAL SIZE
11 lb (5 kg)	6⅜ oz/180 g
22 lb (10 kg)	11 oz/310 g
33 lb (15 kg)	14½ oz/410 g
44 lb (20 kg)	1 lb 2⅛ oz/515 g
66 lb (30 kg)	1 lb 8⅜ oz/690 g
88 lb (40 kg)	1 lb 14⅜ oz/860 g

ENERGY

(per 3½ oz/100 g):	168 Cals

NUTRITIONAL BREAKDOWN PAGE 149

METHOD

Boil the pasta and the zucchini (courgette) in plenty of water and cook at least 5 minutes longer than indicated on the packet: both the pasta and the zucchini (courgette) should be very soft.

Sear the lamb and the heart on a griddle using no fat or oil, taking care not to brown them. If necessary, use a little water to prevent this; it should take around 8–10 minutes. Leave to cool then finely chop.

Serve the pasta and zucchini (courgette) with the meat ragù sauce. Mix with the oil, and add the supplement.

TIP

If you prefer, you can prepare this recipe ahead of time and freeze it. In that case, steam the zucchini (courgette), mash with a fork, and add it to the finely chopped meats. Mix well with the pasta and freeze. Remember, mix it with the oil and add the supplement just before serving.

TWIST

If your dog is a little overweight, substitute the lamb for chicken and, twice a week, with hake, cod, or plaice.

KEEP YOUR DOG'S HEALTH IN MIND

If the zucchini (courgette) is substituted for the same amount of squash, the food will be higher in carotenoids—important nutrients that are also antioxidants.

Couscous with Beef and Vegetables

INGREDIENTS

2 LB 3¼ OZ/1 KG OF FOOD

Couscous	1⅓ cups/225 g
Lean beef	15⅝ oz/445 g
Peas	¾ cup/110 g
Carrots, grated	1½ cups/170 g
Sunflower oil	2 tbsp
Supplement (page 208)	3 tbsp/22 g

WEIGHT

DOG	MEAL SIZE
11 lb (5 kg)	6⅜ oz/180 g
22 lb (10 kg)	10½ oz/300 g
33 lb (15 kg)	14½ oz/410 g
44 lb (20 kg)	1 lb 2 oz/510 g
66 lb (30 kg)	1 lb/8⅜ oz/690 g
88 lb (40 kg)	1 lb/14⅛ oz/855 g

ENERGY

(per 3½ oz/100 g):	170 Cals

NUTRITIONAL BREAKDOWN   PAGE 149

METHOD

Prepare the couscous by boiling it in water for at least 5 minutes longer than indicated on the packet; it should be very soft. Leave to cool.

Sear the beef on a griddle using no fat or oil, taking care not to brown it. If necessary, use a little water to prevent this; it should take around 8–10 minutes. Leave to cool, finely chop and add to the couscous.

Boil the peas in plenty of water for 5 minutes, until cooked. Drain and leave to cool.

Put the couscous and beef in the dog bowl, top with the peas, then the carrots. Lastly, add the oil and supplement.

TIP

To prepare this recipe in advance and freeze it, boil the carrots (cut into rounds) with the peas, and add them to the couscous and the meat. Remember to rinse the couscous under running water, and mix with the oil and supplement just before serving.

TWIST

The couscous can be substituted for the same amount of pasta.

KEEP YOUR DOG'S HEALTH IN MIND

On days when your dog does a lot of exercise or is taken on very demanding walks, add 1 tsp of coconut oil, 2 tsp if your dog weighs over 55 lb (25 kg). It's a great source of energy that's very digestible.

Buckwheat with Berries and Beef

INGREDIENTS

2 LB 3¼ OZ/1 KG OF FOOD

Buckwheat	2 cups/345 g
Lean beef	14⅝ oz/415 g
Spleen	5 oz/140 g
Berries (blueberries, goji berries)	¼ cup/35 g
Corn oil	3½ tbsp
Supplement (page 208)	4½ tbsp/34 g

WEIGHT

DOG	MEAL SIZE
11 lb (5 kg)	5⅛ oz/145 g
22 lb (10 kg)	8⅝ oz/245 g
33 lb (15 kg)	11⅝ oz/330 g
44 lb (20 kg)	14½ oz/410 g
66 lb (30 kg)	1 lb 3¾ oz/560 g
88 lb (40 kg)	1 lb 8⅜ oz/690 g

ENERGY

(per 3½ oz/100 g):	210 Cals

NUTRITIONAL BREAKDOWN PAGE 150

METHOD

Boil the buckwheat in plenty of water and cook for at least 5 minutes longer than indicated on the packet: it should be very soft.

Sear the beef and the spleen on a griddle using no fat or oil, taking care not to brown them. If necessary, use a little water to prevent this; it should take around 5–8 minutes. Leave to cool, then dice the meat and spleen.

Add the buckwheat to the berries and serve with the diced beef and offal. Mix with the oil and add the supplement.

TIP

When the meat is cooked, it can be finely chopped and added to the buckwheat and the berries. Preparing it in this way makes it suitable for freezing, so in this case, remember to mix with the oil and add the supplement just before serving.

TWIST

Spleen is an excellent source of iron; but you can alternate it during the week with lung.

KEEP YOUR DOG'S HEALTH IN MIND

Remember to cook the buckwheat very well as, although it's not a true cereal, it contains substances that need to be well cooked to be easily digested.

ADULT DOGS

Warm Buckwheat with Pork and Berries

INGREDIENTS

2 LB 3¼ OZ/1 KG OF FOOD

Buckwheat	1 cup, plus 1½ tbsp/185 g
Pork neck or shoulder	14 oz/425 g
Pig's heart	14¼ oz/120 g
Corn oil	2 tbsp
Supplement (page 208)	3⅓ tbsp/24 g
Berries (blueberries, goji berries)	¼ cup/30 g
Apple, grated	1¼ cups/185 g

WEIGHT

DOG	MEAL SIZE
11 lb (5 kg)	5⅞ oz/165 g
22 lb (10 kg)	9⅞ oz/280 g
33 lb (15 kg)	13¼ oz/375 g
44 lb (20 kg)	1 lb ½ oz/470 g
66 lb (30 kg)	1 lb 6¼ oz/630 g
88 lb (40 kg)	1 lb 11½ oz/780 g

ENERGY

(per 3½ oz/100 g):	189 Cals

NUTRITIONAL BREAKDOWN   PAGE 150

METHOD

Boil the buckwheat in plenty of water and cook at least 5 minutes longer than indicated on the packet: it should be very soft.

Sear the pork and heart on a griddle using no fat or oil, taking care not to brown them (if necessary, use a little water to prevent this), until cooked. Leave to cool, then cut the meat and offal into little cubes.

Leave the buckwheat to cool completely and add the cubed meat; mix in the oil, add the supplement, and top with the berries and the grated apple.

TIP

You could also steam the buckwheat and the apple (cut into little cubes) and then add the meat and berries; it could then also be frozen. Remember in this case, to mix with the oil and add the supplement just before serving.

TWIST

If your dog isn't crazy about buckwheat, substitute it for the same amount of couscous. If your dog needs a snack between its two meals, give it the correct amount of apple (based on its weight) but remove it from its lunch and dinner.

KEEP YOUR DOG'S HEALTH IN MIND

Goji berries and blueberries, as well as other berries, provide antioxidants which are a natural way of helping avoid your dog's tissues from aging.

Pork and Chicken Stew with Rice

INGREDIENTS

2 LB 3¼ OZ/1 KG OF FOOD

White rice	1 cup/175 g
Carrots	3¾ medium/230 g
Extra-virgin olive oil	1 tbsp
Chicken livers	8⅛ oz/230 g
Chicken breast or thigh, chopped	4¼ oz/120 g
Pork neck or shoulder, chopped	6¼ oz/175 g
Sunflower oil	1 tbsp
Supplement (page 208)	3 tbsp/23 g

WEIGHT

DOG	MEAL SIZE
11 lb (5 kg)	6 oz/170 g
22 lb (10 kg)	10 oz/285 g
33 lb (15 kg)	13¾ oz/390 g
44 lb (20 kg)	1 lb 1¼ oz/490 g
66 lb (30 kg)	1 lb 7¼ oz/660 g
88 lb (40 kg)	1 lb 13 oz/825 g

ENERGY

(per 3½ oz/100 g):	180 Cals

NUTRITIONAL BREAKDOWN   PAGE 151

METHOD

Boil the rice in plenty of water for at least 20 minutes (or at least 5 minutes longer than is indicated on the packet): it should be very soft. Drain and leave to cool.

Also boil the carrots; leave to cool, mash to a purée and add to the rice. Mix in the olive oil and set aside.

Sear the chicken livers on a griddle using no oil, taking care not to brown them (if necessary, use a little water to prevent this). Leave to cool and chop finely.

Steam the chicken and pork for 10 minutes. Leave to cool.

Add the chicken livers to the other meats, mix in the sunflower oil and add the dietary supplement. Serve the stew with the carrot rice.

TIP

If you cook the carrots (cut into little pieces) together with the rice, and cook all the meat on the griddle and then finely chop it, you can combine everything and either refrigerate or freeze it. Just before serving the food, mix it with the two oils and add the supplement.

TWIST

Substitute the pork for the same amount of chicken breast; it will make it lighter.

KEEP YOUR DOG'S HEALTH IN MIND

Extra-virgin olive oil is a natural antioxidant with anti-aging properties.

Barley with Turkey, Beef, and Carrots

INGREDIENTS

2 LB 3¼ OZ/1 KG OF FOOD

Pearl barley	1¼ cups/245 g
Turkey breast	12⅜ oz/350 g
Beef tripe	6¼ oz/175 g
Carrots, grated	1¼ cups/140 g
Corn oil	⅓ cup
Supplement (page 208)	2¾ tbsp/21 g

WEIGHT

DOG	MEAL SIZE
11 lb (5 kg)	5⅛ oz/145 g
22 lb (10 kg)	8½ oz/240 g
33 lb (15 kg)	11½ oz/325 g
44 lb (20 kg)	14 oz/400 g
66 lb (30 kg)	1 lb 3⅜ oz/550 g
88 lb (40 kg)	1½ lb/680 g

ENERGY

(per 3½ oz/100 g):	208 Cals

NUTRITIONAL BREAKDOWN — PAGE 151

METHOD

Boil the pearl barley in plenty of water and cook for at least 5 minutes longer than indicated on the packet: it should be very soft.

Sear the turkey and tripe on a griddle using no fat or oil, taking care not to brown them (if necessary, use a little water to prevent this). Leave to cool, then cut the turkey and tripe into little cubes, and add the supplement.

Add the grated carrots to the barley together with the oil.

Serve the barley and carrots with the meat as soon as it's ready.

TIP

If you refrigerate or freeze it, it's always best to add the oil and dietary supplement just before serving.

TWIST

Instead of using turkey, you can use chicken, and spelt can be substituted for barley. If you'd like to use hulled barley, remember to grind it first.

KEEP YOUR DOG'S HEALTH IN MIND

Beef tripe is available either 'cleaned' or 'green'. From a nutritional point of view, the latter is more complete, but, microbially, carries more risk. It's essential to cook it for this reason.

Rice and Cheese Balls with Stew

INGREDIENTS

2 LB 3¼ OZ/1 KG OF FOOD

White rice	1 cup/190 g
Cheddar cheese, grated	2¼ cups/190 g
Carrots, sliced into rounds	2⅔ cups/315 g
Lean veal, finely diced	9 oz/255 g
Sunflower oil	2 tsp
Supplement (page 208)	3⅓ tbsp/25 g

WEIGHT

DOG	MEAL SIZE
11 lb (5 kg)	5⅝ oz/160 g
22 lb (10 kg)	9½ oz/270 g
33 lb (15 kg)	12⅝ oz/360 g
44 lb (20 kg)	15⅝ oz/445 g
66 lb (30 kg)	1 lb 5⅜ oz/605 g
88 lb (40 kg)	1 lb 10½ oz/760 g

ENERGY

(per 3½ oz/100 g):	196 Cals

NUTRITIONAL BREAKDOWN PAGE 152

METHOD

Boil the rice in plenty of water for at least 20 minutes (or at least 5 minutes longer than is indicated on the packet): it should be very soft. Drain, but make sure it remains moist. Mash it a little, add the cheese, and leave to cool.

Put the carrots and veal into a steamer or colander set over a pan of boiling water. Cover with a lid or tight-fitting foil and steam for 8–10 minutes, until cooked. Once cool, finely chop. Leave to cool then mix in the oil and the dietary supplement.

Shape into lots of little balls rice and cheese mixture and serve with the meat and carrot.

TIP

If you'd like to prepare this in advance and freeze it, finely chop the steamed meat and carrots and add to the rice. Remember if that's what you're going to do, to mix in the oil and add the dietary supplement just before serving.

TWIST

If you're short of time, substitute the rice with the same amount of puffed rice; this doesn't have to be cooked, just rehydrated in water before being mixed with the other ingredients.

KEEP YOUR DOG'S HEALTH IN MIND

Cheddar cheese has very low lactose levels, which means dogs with a mild intolerance can enjoy this meal.

Rosemary Cornmeal with Pork Meatballs

INGREDIENTS

2 LB 3¼ OZ/1 KG OF FOOD

Cornmeal (instant polenta)	1¼ cups/220 g
Ricotta	¾ cup/170 g
Pork neck or shoulder	14 oz/400 g
Zucchini (courgette), diced	1½ cups/170 g
Supplement (page 208)	3 tbsp/23 g
Dried rosemary	1¼ tsp
Sunflower oil	1 tsp

WEIGHT

DOG	MEAL SIZE
11 lb (5 kg)	6¼ oz/175 g
22 lb (10 kg)	10½ oz/300 g
33 lb (15 kg)	14 oz/400 g
44 lb (20 kg)	1 lb 1⅝ oz/500 g
66 lb (30 kg)	1 lb 7⅝ oz/670 g
88 lb (40 kg)	1 lb 13⅝ oz/840 g

ENERGY

(per 3½ oz/100 g):	138 Cals

NUTRITIONAL BREAKDOWN   PAGE 152

METHOD

Prepare the polenta by boiling the cornmeal (instant polenta) in water for at least 5 minutes longer than indicated on the packet. When it's done, add the ricotta and leave to cool.

Sear the pork on a griddle using no fat or oil, taking care not to brown it (if necessary, use a little water to prevent this). Leave to cool and chop finely.

Steam the diced zucchini (courgette). Leave to cool, chop finely and add to the meat together with the dietary supplement.

Flavor the cornmeal with the rosemary and mix in the oil. Mix the meat and vegetables. Shape into lots of little balls; serve on a bed of cornmeal.

TIP

If you'd like to prepare this in advance and freeze it, steam the pork as well (cut into little cubes), then combine the zucchini (courgette) and the pork with the cornmeal. Mix in the oil and add the dietary supplement just before serving.

TWIST

Cottage cheese (fiocchi di latte) can be substituted for the ricotta.

KEEP YOUR DOG'S HEALTH IN MIND

In general, dogs love rosemary, and combined with oil, the aroma becomes very enticing for them.

Beef Roll and Potatoes

INGREDIENTS

2 LB 3¼ OZ/1 KG OF FOOD

White potatoes, diced	2½ cups/365 g
Kefir	1 cup/245 ml
Lean beef	12⅞ oz/365 g
Supplement (page 208)	1⅔ tbsp/12 g
Flaxseed (linseed) oil	2 tsp

WEIGHT

DOG	MEAL SIZE
11 lb (5 kg)	11⅝ oz/330 g
22 lb (10 kg)	1 lb 3⅜ oz/550 g
33 lb (15 kg)	1 lb 10½ oz/750 g
44 lb (20 kg)	2 lb ⅝ oz/925 g
66 lb (30 kg)	2 lb 12½ oz/1.26 kg
88 lb (40 kg)	3 lb 8½ oz/1.6 kg

ENERGY

(per 3½ oz/100 g):	91 Cals

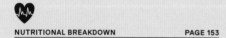

NUTRITIONAL BREAKDOWN   PAGE 153

METHOD

Put the potatoes into a steamer or colander set over a pan of boiling water. Cover with a lid or tight-fitting foil and steam for 8–10 minutes, until cooked. Once cool, finely chop. Leave to cool, mash with a fork and add the kefir.

Sear the beef on a griddle using no fat or oil, taking care not to brown it (if necessary, use a little water to prevent this). Leave to cool, chop finely and combine with the potatoes.

Finish by adding the supplement and oil then shape into a roll and cut into slices.

TIP

If you are short of time, cut the beef into little cubes and steam together with the potatoes. Drain and chop everything finely. Finish off by adding the kefir and the supplement and oil; if you are going to freeze it, add the oil and supplement when you're about to serve it.

TWIST

If you wish, substitute half of the kefir (by weight) with ricotta made from cow's milk, sheep's milk, or a combination of the two.

KEEP YOUR DOG'S HEALTH IN MIND

Kefir is a good source of probiotics, which help stimulate the immune system. It's a great and healthy concentrate, even suitable for lactose-intolerant dogs.

Pasta with Squash and Cornmeal

INGREDIENTS

2 LB 3¼ OZ/1 KG OF FOOD

Durum wheat semolina pasta	4 oz/115 g
Squash, diced	1⅔ cups/235 g
Cornmeal (instant polenta)	⅔ cup/115 g
Lean veal, finely chopped	1 lb ⅜ oz/465 g
Supplement (page 208)	4½ tbsp/35 g
Corn oil	3½ tsp

WEIGHT

DOG	MEAL SIZE
11 lb (5 kg)	6¼ oz/170 g
22 lb (10 kg)	10¼ oz/290 g
33 lb (15 kg)	13¾ oz/395 g
44 lb (20 kg)	1 lb 1⅛ oz/485 g
66 lb (30 kg)	1 lb 7⅛ oz/655 g
88 lb (40 kg)	1 lb 12⅞ oz/820 g

ENERGY

(per 3½ oz/100 g):	174 Cals

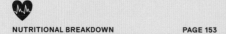

NUTRITIONAL BREAKDOWN	PAGE 153

METHOD

Boil the pasta and the squash in plenty of water and cook at least 5 minutes longer than indicated on the packet: they should both be very soft.

Prepare the cornmeal (instant polenta) by boiling it in water for at least 5 minutes longer than indicated on the packet, then leave to cool.

Put the veal into a steamer or colander set over a pan of boiling water. Cover with a lid or tight-fitting foil and steam for 8–10 minutes, until cooked. Leave to cool then combine with the polenta and add the supplement.

Mix the pasta and the squash with the oil and serve with the cornmeal.

TIP

If you are going to freeze it, cut up the cooked pasta and squash and chop the steamed meat finely. Combine everything with the cornmeal and, when about to serve, mix with the oil and add the supplement.

TWIST

In the summer, substitute the same amount of zucchini (courgette) for squash.

KEEP YOUR DOG'S HEALTH IN MIND

Veal has fewer trace minerals than beef, but it is very low in fat.

Beef Stew with Rice and Apple

INGREDIENTS

2 LB 3¼ OZ/1 KG OF FOOD

White rice	½ cup/95 g
Parmesan cheese, grated	1 cup/95 g
Pork fat (lard)	2 tbsp/25 g
Aged beef	1 lb ½ oz/470 g
Sunflower oil	3½ tsp
Flaxseed (linseed) oil	3½ tsp
Salmon oil	3½ tsp
Supplement (page 208)	3⅓ tbsp/24 g
Apples, unpeeled, diced	2⅛ cups/235 g

WEIGHT

DOG	MEAL SIZE
11 lb (5 kg)	7⅜ oz/210 g
22 lb (10 kg)	12¾ oz/360 g
33 lb (15 kg)	1 lb 1 oz/485 g
44 lb (20 kg)	1 lb 5 oz/600 g
66 lb (30 kg)	1 lb 12 oz/810 g
88 lb (40 kg)	2 lb 3 oz/1 kg

ENERGY

(per 3½ oz/100 g):	230 Cals

NUTRITIONAL BREAKDOWN   PAGE 154

METHOD

Boil the rice in plenty of water for at least 20 minutes (or 5 minutes longer than the cooking time indicated on the packet); it should be very soft. Drain, leave to cool, and add the cheese and pork fat.

Sear the beef in a dry griddle pan, without browning it (add a little water if necessary). Let cool, then cut into squares.

Mix the meat with the oils and dietary supplement, and serve with the rice mixed with the apple.

TIP

You can also cut the beef into small pieces and steam together with the diced apples, then add to the rice and finish with the cheese. If you want to freeze this dish, add the oils and dietary supplement at the last minute before serving.

TWIST

If the beef is already fatty, there's no need to add the pork fat.

KEEP YOUR DOG'S HEALTH IN MIND

The omega-3 fatty acids contained in the vegetable oils in this recipe have a positive effect on your dog's physical performance.

Beef with Vegetables and Ginger

INGREDIENTS

2 LB 3¼ OZ/1 KG OF FOOD

14–15% fat aged beef	14 oz/400 g
Carrots, diced	1¾ cups/165 g
Zucchini (courgette), diced	1½ cups/165 g
White rice	1¼ cups/190 g
Sunflower oil	3 tsp
Coconut oil	3 tsp
Flaxseed (linseed) oil	5 tsp
Supplement (page 208)	2¼ tbsp/16 g
Parmesan cheese, grated	⅓ cup/30 g
Ground ginger	1 tsp

WEIGHT

DOG	MEAL SIZE
11 lb (5 kg)	6½ oz/185 g
22 lb (10 kg)	11 oz/310 g
33 lb (15 kg)	15 oz/425 g
44 lb (20 kg)	1 lb 1½ oz/520 g
66 lb (30 kg)	1 lb 5 oz/705 g
88 lb (40 kg)	1 lb 9 oz/890 g

ENERGY

(per 3½ oz/100 g):	221 Cals

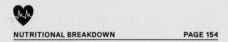

NUTRITIONAL BREAKDOWN PAGE 154

METHOD

Cut the beef and its fat into small cubes, arrange them in a single layer inside a steamer, and steam for 20–30 minutes. Use a fork to check the meat is cooked through. You could use a microwave to halve the cooking time: put the cubes of meat into a container, cover with plastic wrap (clingfilm), perforated a few times, and cook at 850 W for 8–10 minutes.

Steam the vegetables for 7–8 minutes. If you want to make a purée, cook for a few more minutes, then mash them with a fork.

Boil the rice for about 2 minutes longer than the cooking time indicated on the packet, then drain and rinse to remove the starch. Leave them to cool.

Mix the meat with the rice and vegetables. Add the oils and dietary supplement, and finally the grated cheese and ground ginger. Mix well before serving.

TWIST

If the meat's fresh and you're certain of its source you can serve it raw, as a tartare.

KEEP YOUR DOG'S HEALTH IN MIND

If your dog suffers from kidney problems, replace the white rice with the same amount of low-protein pasta and the sunflower oil with krill oil.

ADULT DOGS

Multi-Layered Brown Rice

INGREDIENTS

2 LB 3¼ OZ/1 KG OF FOOD

Skinless turkey breast	6 oz/170 g
Lean veal	6 oz/170 g
Salmon, chopped	6 oz/170 g
Brown rice	1⅔ cups/305 g
Squash, diced	1 cup/135 g
Corn oil	1½ tbsp
Supplement (page 208)	3⅔ tbsp/27 g

WEIGHT

DOG	MEAL SIZE
11 lb (5 kg)	5½ oz/155 g
22 lb (10 kg)	9⅛ oz/260 g
33 lb (15 kg)	12⅝ oz/360 g
44 lb (20 kg)	15½ cups/440 g
66 lb (30 kg)	1 lb 5⅛ oz/600 g
88 lb (40 kg)	1 lb 10½ oz/750 g

ENERGY

(per 3½ oz/100 g):	190 Cals

NUTRITIONAL BREAKDOWN	PAGE 155

METHOD

Boil the rice in plenty of water for at least 20 minutes (or at least 5 minutes longer than is indicated): it should be very soft. Drain and leave to cool.

Put the salmon and squash into opposite sides of a steamer or colander set over a pan of boiling water. Cover with a lid or tight-fitting foil and steam for 8–10 minutes, until cooked.

Sear the turkey and the veal on a griddle using no fat or oil, taking care not to brown them (if necessary, use a little water to prevent this). Leave to cool and chop.

Combine the rice and the salmon and add the dietary supplement.

Mix the oil with the squash, and make a first layer with half of the rice mixture. Cover with a layer of squash, then a layer of turkey, another layer of rice, and finish with a layer of veal.

TIP

If freezing, steam the fish and meat together, then chop finely. Boil the rice with the squash, then add to the meat and fish. Mix with the oil and supplement just before serving.

TWIST

The salmon can be replaced with trout.

KEEP YOUR DOG'S HEALTH IN MIND

In general, freshwater fish has more fat, so you can't swap this out for sea fish.

Stew with Beans, Rice, and Berries

INGREDIENTS

2 LB 3¼ OZ/1 KG OF FOOD

Puffed rice	12 cups/170 g
Chicken breast or thigh, chopped	9⅛ oz/260 g
Green beans, diced	1¾ cups/200 g
Lean veal	9⅛ oz/260 g
Supplement (page 208)	3 tbsp/23 g
Berries (blueberries, goji berries)	3 tbsp/30 g
Sunflower oil	3½ tbsp

WEIGHT

DOG	MEAL SIZE
11 lb (5 kg)	6¼ oz/175 g
22 lb (10 kg)	10⅜ oz/295 g
33 lb (15 kg)	14 oz/400 g
44 lb (20 kg)	1 lb 1½ oz/490 g
66 lb (30 kg)	1 lb 7½ oz/665 g
88 lb (40 kg)	1 lb 13¼ oz/830 g

ENERGY

(per 3½ oz/100 g):	174 Cals

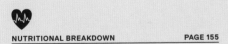

NUTRITIONAL BREAKDOWN   PAGE 155

METHOD

Soak the puffed rice in water. Meanwhile, steam the chicken and the green beans, making sure there are no bones or splinters in the meat.

Sear the veal on a griddle using no fat or oil, taking care not to brown it (if necessary, use a little water to prevent this). Leave to cool and chop finely.

Combine the chicken and the beans with the veal and add the dietary supplement.

Combine the puffed rice and the berries, mix in the oil and serve it with the meat and vegetable stew.

TIP

If you are short of time, steam all the meat and the green beans (all cut into little pieces) and add to the puffed rice and the berries. If you're feeding your dog now, mix in the oil and add the dietary supplement; but, if you're going to freeze the food, add these just before serving.

TWIST

If you like, you can use all chicken or all veal as long as the total weight of meat remains the same.

KEEP YOUR DOG'S HEALTH IN MIND

Berries are high in natural antioxidants, vitamins and mineral salts. Goji berries, in particular, have many attributes; they help keep your dog's coat shiny and its eyesight sharp, among other benefits.

Surf and Turf with Spirulina

INGREDIENTS

2 LB 3¼ OZ/1 KG OF FOOD

Fatty beef	4¾ oz/135 g
Beef heart	3⅛ oz/90 g
Beef tripe	4¾ oz/135 g
Carrots, grated	2 cups/230 g
Pumpkin seed flour	1 tbsp
Spirulina powder	4 tsp/9 g
Trout	4¾ oz/135 g
Green beans	1¼ cups/140 g
Sunflower oil	2 tbsp, plus 2 tsp
Supplement (page 208)	1¼ tbsp/9 g
Parmesan cheese, grated	½ cup/45 g
Pine nuts	3 tbsp/25 g

WEIGHT

DOG	MEAL SIZE
11 lb (5 kg)	7¾ oz/220 g
22 lb (10 kg)	12 ⅞ oz/365 g
33 lb (15 kg)	1 lb 2 oz/510 g
44 lb (20 kg)	1 lb 6 oz/625 g
66 lb (30 kg)	1 lb 14 oz/850 g
88 lb (40 kg)	2 lb 3¼ oz/1 kg

ENERGY

(per 3½ oz/100 g):	173 Cals

NUTRITIONAL BREAKDOWN   PAGE 156

METHOD

Sear the beef, heart, and tripe in a dry griddle pan, taking care not to brown them (add a little water if necessary). Leave to cool, cut into dice, and combine with the carrots, flour, and spirulina.

Put the fish and beans into opposite sides of a steamer or colander set over a pan of boiling water. Cover with a lid or tight-fitting foil and steam for 8–10 minutes, until cooked. Mix with the oil, supplment, and grated cheese, and finish with the whole pine nuts.

Serve the meat alongside the fish.

TIP

If you want to freeze this dish in portions, remember that it's best to only add the oil and dietary supplement just before serving.

TWIST

Wild trout is much more difficult to find than farmed trout, but wild has a much higher nutritional value.

KEEP YOUR DOG'S HEALTH IN MIND

Pine nuts are a major source of magnesium, a mineral that's good for soothing muscle tension and cramps.

ADULT DOGS

Tartare Trio

INGREDIENTS

2 LB 3¼ OZ/1 KG OF FOOD

Chicken giblets, finely chopped	2¼ oz/150 g
Carrots, grated	1¾ cups/205 g
Supplement (page 208)	2⅔ tbsp/20 g
Spirulina powder	3 tsp/15 g
Peas	1 cup/150 g
Lean beef, finely chopped	4¼ oz/150 g
Rabbit, finely chopped	4 oz/140 g
Corn oil	1 tbsp
Salmon, finely chopped	3⅛ oz/90 g
Pine nuts	3 tbsp/25 g
Pumpkin seeds	1½ tbsp
Salmon oil	1 tbsp

WEIGHT

DOG	MEAL SIZE
11 lb (5 kg)	7¼ oz/205 g
22 lb (10 kg)	11¾ oz/335 g
33 lb (15 kg)	1 lb/455 g
44 lb (20 kg)	1 lb 3⅞ oz/565 g
66 lb (30 kg)	1 lb 11 oz/765 g
88 lb (40 kg)	2 lb 1⅝ oz/955 g

ENERGY

(per 3½ oz/100 g):	159 Cals

NUTRITIONAL BREAKDOWN · PAGE 156

METHOD

Combine the giblets with the carrots, dietary supplement, and spirulina.

Blanch the peas. Mix the beef and rabbit tartare with the peas, and mix in the corn oil.

Finish the salmon tartare with the pine nuts and pumpkin seeds, and mix in the salmon oil.

Serve the trio of tartares side by side.

TWIST

You could replace the salmon with another type of freshwater fish such as trout or perch. If you're not sure of where the meat or fish were sourced, it's a good idea to sear it in a griddle pan.

KEEP YOUR DOG'S HEALTH IN MIND

Spirulina is an algae containing omega-3 and minerals, which strengthen your dog's immune system, help it to regain energy after convalescence, and improve the look of its skin and coat.

Lamb and Cod with Egg

INGREDIENTS

2 LB 3¼ OZ/1 KG OF FOOD

Cod, cut into small pieces	6⅜ oz/180 g
Lamb	3¾ oz/105 g
Salmon oil	1 tbsp
Spirulina powder	1 generous tbsp/18 g
Pumpkin seeds, toasted and ground	3 tbsp
Carrots, diced	1¾ cups/250 g
Peas	1¼ cups/180 g
Eggs	¾ cup/190 g
Pine nuts	3 tbsp/18 g
Supplement (page 208)	2 tbsp/14 g
Corn oil	1 tbsp

WEIGHT

DOG	MEAL SIZE
11 lb (5 kg)	9⅞ oz/280 g
22 lb (10 kg)	1 lb ¾ oz/475 g
33 lb (15 kg)	1 lb 6½ oz/640 g
44 lb (20 kg)	1 lb 11¾ oz/790 g
66 lb (30 kg)	2 lb 6¾ oz/1.1 kg
88 lb (40 kg)	2 lb 15¼ oz/1.34 kg

ENERGY

(per 3½ oz/100 g):	111 Cals

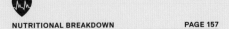

NUTRITIONAL BREAKDOWN PAGE 157

METHOD

Put the cod into the steamer or colander set over a pan of boiling water. Cover with a lid or tight-fitting foil and steam for 8–10 minutes, until cooked. Leave to cool and finely chop.

Sear the lamb in a dry griddle pan, taking care not to brown it. Cool and finely chop.

Mix the chopped meat and fish, then add the salmon oil, spirulina, and ground pumpkin seeds. Shape the mixture into quenelles, using all of the mixture.

Boil the carrots, together with the peas. Soft-boil the eggs to achieve firm whites and runny yolks.

Add the nuts to the peas and carrots, then the supplement, and mix in the corn oil.

Peel the eggs and serve on a bed of vegetables with the quenelles.

TIP

If you want to store this dish in the refrigerator, you can do so with the boiled eggs (they will keep for several days in the refrigerator). However, if you want to freeze the meal, boil the eggs just before serving.

TWIST

You can replace the cod with hake or plaice.

KEEP YOUR DOG'S HEALTH IN MIND

You can keep the pumpkin seeds whole and serve as a healthy snack.

SENIOR DOGS

Rice, Egg, and Vegetable Croquettes

INGREDIENTS

2 LB 3¼ OZ/1 KG OF FOOD

White rice	1⅓ cups/255 g
Eggs	1⅓ cups/340 g
Pumpkin, diced	1 cup/125 g
Parmesan cheese, grated	¾ cup/65 g
Carrots	2 medium/125 g
Coconut oil	1 tbsp
Brewer's yeast (or Marmite)	4½ tbsp/25 g
Sunflower oil	4 tsp
Supplement (page 208)	3⅓ tbsp/25 g

WEIGHT

DOG	MEAL SIZE
11 lb (5 kg)	5⅝ oz/160 g
22 lb (10 kg)	9⅛ oz/260 g
33 lb (15 kg)	12½ oz/355 g
44 lb (20 kg)	1 lb/450 g
66 lb (30 kg)	1 lb 5½ oz/610 g
88 lb (40 kg)	1 lb 10 oz/740 g

ENERGY

(per 3½ oz/100 g):	195 Cals

NUTRITIONAL BREAKDOWN   PAGE 160

METHOD

Boil the rice in plenty of water for 5 minutes longer than the cooking time indicated on the packet; it should be soft.

Put the pumpkin into the steamer or colander set over a pan of boiling water. Cover with a lid or tight-fitting foil and steam for 8–10 minutes, until cooked. Leave it to cool and blend to a purée. Mix with the eggs, rice, cheese, and yeast, and shape into croquettes.

Line a baking pan with baking parchment and arrange the croquettes, spaced well apart, in it. Bake in the oven until golden, then leave to cool.

Wash and cut the carrots into thin strips, mix with the oils and supplement. Serve the croquettes on a bed of carrot strips.

TIP

These croquettes are convenient to carry around. You could also steam the carrots with the pumpkin then mix them into the mixture. If you do that, remember to add the supplement when you're about to serve, because they shouldn't be cooked.

TWIST

You can replace the Parmesan cheese with aged pecorino cheese.

KEEP YOUR DOG'S HEALTH IN MIND

The properties of brewer's yeast, particularly its high B-group vitamin content, make it an excellent supplement for skin and coat health.

Pasta with Smashed Eggs

INGREDIENTS

2 LB 3¼ OZ/1 KG OF FOOD

Wholegrain pasta	6 oz/170 g
Butter	5 tsp
Pumpkin, finely diced	1½ cups/170 g
Carrots, finely diced	1⅛ cups/170 g
Beef lung, finely chopped	6 oz/170 g
Eggs	4 extra large/235 g
Coconut oil	1 tbsp
Flaxseed (linseed) oil	1 tbsp
Salmon oil	5 tsp
Supplement (page 208)	2¼ tbsp/17 g

WEIGHT

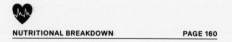

DOG	MEAL SIZE
11 lb (5 kg)	6¼ oz/175 g
22 lb (10 kg)	10¼ oz/290 g
33 lb (15 kg)	14¼ oz/405 g
44 lb (20 kg)	1 lb 1½ oz/495 g
66 lb (30 kg)	1 lb 7¾ oz/675 g
88 lb (40 kg)	1 lb 13⅝ oz/840 g

ENERGY

(per 3½ oz/100 g):	170 Cals

NUTRITIONAL BREAKDOWN — PAGE 160

METHOD

Boil the pasta in plenty of water for 5 minutes longer than the cooking time indicated on the packet. Drain, setting aside a few tbsp of cooking liquid, then add the butter and leave to cool.

Put the vegetables and beef into the steamer or colander set over a pan of boiling water. Cover with a lid or tight-fitting foil and steam for 8–10 minutes, until cooked. Blend the vegetables to a creamy consistency and stir into the pasta, diluting with a little of the pasta cooking liquid. Mix in the beef.

Soft-boil the eggs and let them cool. Peel, cut into pieces, and smash with a fork until crumbled. Mix with the oils and sprinkle the mixture over the pasta.

Finish with the supplement and serve warm.

TIP

If you want to freeze the dish, remember to rinse the pasta in cold water after cooking to prevent the formation of resistant starch.

TWIST

You can replace the wholegrain pasta with wholegrain bread, increasing the amount by 20 percent.

KEEP YOUR DOG'S HEALTH IN MIND

The medium-chain triglycerides (MCT) contained in the coconut oil are an important source of energy for a dog's neurons.

Rice Zuccotto with Turkey

INGREDIENTS

2 LB 3¼ OZ/1 KG OF FOOD

Skinless turkey breast	10 oz/285 g
White rice	¾ cup/150 g
Chicory	4 heads/260 g
Green beans	2⅓ cups/260 g
Corn oil	1 tbsp
Supplement (page 208)	2⅔ tbsp/18 g

WEIGHT

DOG	MEAL SIZE
11 lb (5 kg)	8⅛ oz/230 g
22 lb (10 kg)	13½ oz/385 g
33 lb (15 kg)	1 lb 2⅝ oz/520 g
44 lb (20 kg)	1 lb 7 oz/650 g
66 lb (30 kg)	1 lb 15 oz/880 g
88 lb (40 kg)	2 lb 6¾ oz/1.1 kg

ENERGY

(per 3½ oz/100 g):	132 Cals

NUTRITIONAL BREAKDOWN PAGE 161

METHOD

Boil the rice in plenty of water for at least 20 minutes (or 5 minutes longer than the cooking time indicated on the packet); it should be very soft.

Cut the turkey into small pieces (to reduce the cooking time) and steam. Leave to cool and mix with the rice.

Boil the chicory and beans in plenty of water and drain. Blend to a purée, mix in the oil, and leave to cool.

Add the supplement to the rice and turkey mixture, put into a lightly greased bowl, and press down well so that it's compact. Then turn out the zuccotto. Add the vegetable purée around it and serve.

TIP

You could steam the vegetables with the turkey, then mix with the rice and freeze. If you're going to do so, add the oil and supplement at the last minute before serving.

TWIST

You can replace the green beans with lentils, reducing the weight by two-thirds.

KEEP YOUR DOG'S HEALTH IN MIND

Chicory is an excellent natural prebiotic. It's an important source of inulin, a substance that stimulates the good bacteria in the intestines.

Turmeric Rice with Turkey

INGREDIENTS

2 LB 3¼ OZ/1 KG OF FOOD

Brown rice	1⅛ cups/215 g
Turmeric	1 tsp
Skinless turkey breast, chopped	11¼ oz/320 g
White potatoes, diced	1½ cups/425 g
Corn oil	1 tbsp
Supplement (page 208)	2¾ tbsp/21 g

WEIGHT

DOG	MEAL SIZE
11 lb (5 kg)	6¾ oz/190 g
22 lb (10 kg)	11 oz/315 g
33 lb (15 kg)	1 lb/425 g
44 lb (20 kg)	1 lb 2½ oz/530 g
66 lb (30 kg)	1 lb 9 oz/720 g
88 lb (40 kg)	1 lb 15 oz/890 g

ENERGY

(per 3½ oz/100 g):	161 Cals

NUTRITIONAL BREAKDOWN   PAGE 161

METHOD

Boil the brown rice with the turmeric in plenty of water for at least 20 minutes (or at least 5 minutes longer than is indicated on the packet): it should be very soft. Drain and leave to cool.

Steam the turkey and potatoes (cut into little pieces to shorten the cooking time), making sure there are no bones or splinters in the meat. Leave to cool.

Mix the brown rice with the oil, combine with the meat and potatoes, then add the supplement just before serving.

TIP

The meat and potatoes can be steamed together with the brown rice and turmeric then frozen. Mix with the oil and add the supplement only when you're about to serve it.

TWIST

If your dog likes the taste of turmeric, you can add it at the end, when you're about to serve it.

KEEP YOUR DOG'S HEALTH IN MIND

Turmeric is a good ally to your dog's health because it's a concentrate of antioxidants.

Vegetable Cream with Croutons

INGREDIENTS

2 LB 3¼ OZ/1 KG OF FOOD

Pumpkin or squash, diced	¾ cup/95 g
Carrots, diced	¾ cup/95 g
Turkey thigh, skinless	8⅛ oz/230 g
Rolled oats	⅓ cup, plus 2 tbsp/40 g
Plain nonfat yogurt	1½ cup/370 ml
White bread	3 slices/90 g
Coconut oil	1 tbsp
Salmon oil	1 tbsp
Flaxseed (linseed) oil	4 tsp
Supplement (page 208)	3 tbsp/23 g

WEIGHT

DOG	MEAL SIZE
11 lb (5 kg)	7½ oz/215 g
22 lb (10 kg)	13 oz/370 g
33 lb (15 kg)	1 lb 1¾ oz/490 g
44 lb (20 kg)	1 lb 5½ oz/610 g
66 lb (30 kg)	1 lb 13¼ oz/830 g
88 lb (40 kg)	2 lb 3¼ oz/1 kg

ENERGY

(per 3½ oz/100 g):	137 Cals

NUTRITIONAL BREAKDOWN   PAGE 162

METHOD

Cook the diced pumpkin or squash and carrots in a pan with a little water, then blend to a creamy consistency and leave to cool.

Sear the turkey in a dry griddle pan, taking care not to brown it, until cooked. Let cool, then finely chop.

Reconstitute the oats in lukewarm water and mix with the yogurt. Cut the bread into cubes and dry out in the oven to make croutons.

Add the meat and yogurt to the pumpkin and carrot cream, mix well, and top with the croutons. Mix in the oils, add the dietary supplement, and serve.

TIP

You can also serve your dog the yogurt with oats as a snack.

TWIST

The turkey can be replaced with the same amount of guinea fowl.

KEEP YOUR DOG'S HEALTH IN MIND

The selenium in rolled oats is an essential trace mineral that combats the free radicals that cause aging.

SENIOR DOGS

Tapioca with Pork and Carrots

INGREDIENTS

2 LB 3¼ OZ/1 KG OF FOOD

Tapioca flour	1¾ cups/240 g
Pork neck or shoulder	14¾ oz/420 g
Pig's liver	4¼ oz/120 g
Supplement (page 208)	3⅓ tbsp/24 g
Sunflower oil	1 tbsp
Carrots, grated	1⅔ cups/180 g

WEIGHT

DOG	MEAL SIZE
11 lb (5 kg)	5⅞ oz/165 g
22 lb (10 kg)	9⅞ oz/280 g
33 lb (15 kg)	13⅜ oz/380 g
44 lb (20 kg)	1 lb ¾ oz/475 g
66 lb (30 kg)	1 lb 6½ oz/640 g
88 lb (40 kg)	1¾ lb/800 g

ENERGY

(per 3½ oz/100 g):	180 Cals

NUTRITIONAL BREAKDOWN PAGE 162

METHOD

Boil the tapioca in water for at least 5 minutes longer than is indicated on the packet, then leave to cool.

Sear the pork and the liver on a griddle using no fat or oil, taking care not to brown them (if necessary, use a little water to prevent this). Leave to cool, cut into little cubes and add the dietary supplement.

Serve the tapioca mixed with the oil, and topped with the meat and the carrots.

TIP

If you'd like to freeze it, cut up the meat when it's been cooked, steam the carrots (cut into rounds) then mash with a fork. Combine with the tapioca and mix with the oil and add the dietary supplement just before serving.

TWIST

A good variation is to swap the liver for the same weight of soft-boiled eggs twice a week.

KEEP YOUR DOG'S HEALTH IN MIND

Be careful not to overdo it with the liver and to always follow the amounts indicated in these recipes: too much can be dangerous for your dog.

Quinoa with Squash and Lamb Ragù

INGREDIENTS

2 LB 3¼ OZ/1 KG OF FOOD

Quinoa	2⅓ cups/395 g
Squash, finely diced	1 cup/155 g
Corn oil	1½ tbsp
Lamb	13½ oz/395 g
Supplement (page 208)	4 tbsp/31 g

WEIGHT

DOG	MEAL SIZE
11 lb (5 kg)	4⅜ oz/125 g
22 lb (10 kg)	7½ oz/215 g
33 lb (15 kg)	10¼ oz/290 g
44 lb (20 kg)	12⅝ oz/360 g
66 lb (30 kg)	1 lb 1¼ oz/490 g
88 lb (40 kg)	1 lb 5⅜ oz/605 g

ENERGY

(per 3½ oz/100 g):	237 Cals

NUTRITIONAL BREAKDOWN   PAGE 163

METHOD

Wash the quinoa well and boil it, together with the squash in plenty water for at least 5 minutes longer than indicated on the packet. Drain the squash and quinoa, leave to cool and mix in the oil.

Sear the lamb on a griddle using no fat or oil, taking care not to brown it (if necessary, use a little water to prevent this). Leave to cool, chop finely and add the dietary supplement.

Serve the quinoa with squash together with the lamb ragù sauce.

TIP

If you'd like to freeze it, remember to add the oil and dietary supplement when you're about to serve it.

TWIST

You can substitute mutton for the lamb: this is an economical meat and is particularly appreciated by dogs.

KEEP YOUR DOG'S HEALTH IN MIND

Quinoa is a pseudocereal and is perfect for dogs that are intolerant to wheat; it is also high in protein and fiber. Remember to always wash it before cooking as it can have a bitter taste that dogs do not always like.

SENIOR DOGS

SENIOR DOGS

Coconut-Scented Couscous

INGREDIENTS

2 LB 3¼ OZ/1 KG OF FOOD

Couscous	2⅛ cups/365 g
Coconut oil	1 tbsp
Pork neck or shoulder	15⅞ oz/450 g
Chicken giblets	4¼ oz/120 g
Sunflower oil	1 tbsp
Supplement (page 208)	4⅓ tbsp/33 g

WEIGHT

DOG	MEAL SIZE
11 lb (5 kg)	4⅜ oz/125 g
22 lb (10 kg)	7¼ oz/205 g
33 lb (15 kg)	10 oz/285 g
44 lb (20 kg)	12⅜ oz/350 g
66 lb (30 kg)	1 lb ½ oz/470 g
88 lb (40 kg)	1 lb 4⅝ oz/585 g

ENERGY

(per 3½ oz/100 g):	244 Cals

NUTRITIONAL BREAKDOWN   PAGE 163

METHOD

Prepare the couscous and cook it for at least 5 minutes longer than is indicated on the packet: it should be very soft. Leave it to cool, then mix it with the coconut oil.

Sear the pork and the chicken giblets on a griddle using no fat or oil, taking care not to brown them; if necessary, use a little water to prevent this. Leave to cool, then cut the meat and giblets into little cubes.

Mix in the sunflower oil, add the dietary supplement and serve with the coconut-scented couscous.

TIP

If you'd like to prepare this in advance and freeze it, steam the meat, chop it finely and add it to the couscous. Mix it with the two oils and add the dietary supplement just before serving.

TWIST

Cook the couscous in stock; this will make the food even more appetizing to your pet.

KEEP YOUR DOG'S HEALTH IN MIND

As dogs get older, their sense of smell tends to wane; to stimulate their appetite, it becomes very important to offer your pet meals that smell good.

NUTRITIONAL VALUES

How to Use This Section

In the recipe section of this book, you'll find calorie content, portion sizes, and helpful information about how and why each recipe is good for your pet. In this nutritional value section, there is an even more detailed breakdown of what goes into every meal served, along with a helpful infographic illustration to show the percentage of minerals, protein, fats, carbohydrate, and fiber in every 3½ oz (100g) of food.

A FEW THINGS TO NOTE

You'll find that there are four charts for every puppy recipe, as opposed to one—this is because portion sizes are based on the adult weight of the dog, and then subsequently the growth stage of the puppy.

Quantities of each ingredient refer to the prepared and cooked amount. As previously stated, these recipes were created using metric grams, so this is the most accurate measurement to follow, however US imperial measurements are also included.

The infographic illustrations provide a useful cross reference to the 'Keep Your Dog's Health in Mind' details in each recipe, along with the icons highlighting dietary requirements, such as grain free, high protein, and lighter meals for less energetic dogs. At a glance, you can see how each meal is balanced for that purpose.

HOW TO USE THIS SECTION

PUPPY
NUTRITION

Carrot Risotto with Seared Beef

DAILY QUANTITY

INGREDIENTS	ADULT WEIGHT: 88 LB/40 KG					
Dog Weight	11 lb /5 kg	22 lb /10 kg	33 lb /15 kg	44 lb /20 kg	66 lb /30 kg	77 lb /35 kg
Beef	7⅜ oz /210 g	11⅝ oz /330 g	14 oz /400 g	1 lb ⅛ oz /460 g	1 lb 5⅞ oz /620 g	1 lb 3⅜ oz /550 g
White rice	⅜ cup /80 g	⅔ cup /125 g	⅞ cup /155 g	1 cup /175 g	1¼ cups /235 g	⅛ cup /210 g
Spleen	2 ½ oz /70 g	3⅞ oz /110 g	4¾ oz /135 g	5½ oz /155 g	7¼ oz /205 g	6½ oz /185 g
Carrots, sliced	⅜ cup /50 g	⅔ cup /80 g	¾ cup /95 g	⅞ cup /110 g	1¼ cups /145 g	1⅛ cups /130 g
Salmon oil	½ tsp	⅔ tsp	⅞ tsp	1 tsp	1¼ tsp	1 tsp
Flaxseed (linseed) oil	2 tsp	1 tbsp	4 tsp	4½ tsp	2¼ tbsp	2 tbsp
Supplement	1 tbsp + 1 tsp/10 g	1 tbsp + ⅓ tsp/16 g	2 tbsp + 2⅓ tsp/19 g	3 tbsp + ⅓ tsp/22 g	Scant 4 tbsp/29 g	3 tbsp + 1⅓ tsp/ 26 g

NUTRITION PER 3½ OZ/100 G

MACRONUTRIENTS

■ MINERALS ■ PROTEINS ■ FIBER
■ FATS ■ CARBOHYDRATES

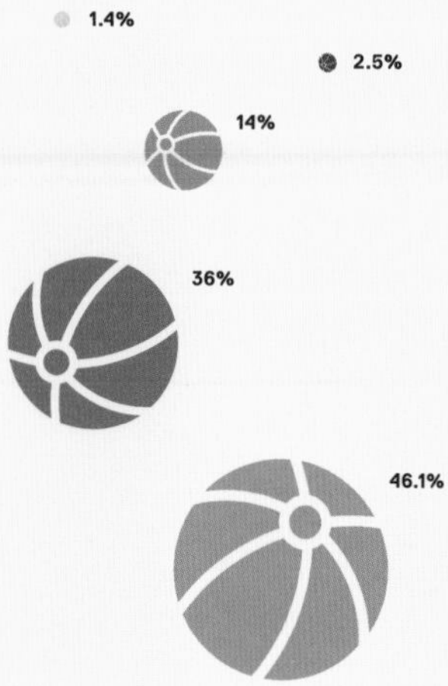
1.4%
2.5%
14%
36%
46.1%

DAILY QUANTITY

INGREDIENTS	ADULT WEIGHT: 55 LB/25 KG			
Dog Weight	11 lb /5 kg	22 lb /10 kg	33 lb /15 kg	44 lb /20 kg
Beef	7⅜ oz /210 g	10⅜ oz /295 g	12⅞ oz /365 g	12⅞ oz /365 g
White rice	⅜ cup /80 g	⅔ cup /115 g	¾ cup /140 g	¾ cup /140 g
Spleen	2½ oz /70 g	3½ oz /100 g	4¼ oz /120 g	4¼ oz /120 g
Carrots, sliced	⅜ cup /50 g	½ cup /70 g	¾ cup /85 g	¾ cup /85 g
Salmon oil	½ tsp	⅔ tsp	⅞ tsp	⅞ tsp
Flaxseed (linseed) oil	2 tsp	1 tbsp	1¼ tbsp	1¼ tbsp
Supplement	1 tbsp + 1 tsp/10 g	Scant 2 tbsp/14 g	2 tbsp + ¾ tsp/17 g	2 tbsp + ¾ tsp/17 g

NUTRITION PER 3½ OZ/100 G

MACRONUTRIENTS

■ MINERALS ■ PROTEINS ■ FIBER
■ FATS ■ CARBOHYDRATES

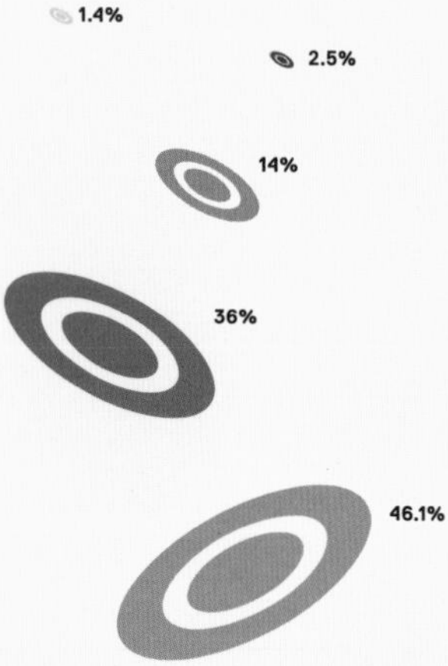
1.4%
2.5%
14%
36%
46.1%

DAILY QUANTITY

INGREDIENTS	ADULT WEIGHT: 22 LB/10 KG		
Dog Weight	6 lb 6 oz /3 kg	13 lb 2 oz /6 kg	20 lb /9 kg
Beef	5 ⅛ oz /145 g	7¼ oz /205 g	7¾ oz /220 g
White rice	¼ cup /55 g	⅜ cup / 75 g	½ cup /85 g
Spleen	1¾ oz /50 g	2½ oz /70 g	2⅝ oz /75 g
Carrots, sliced	⅜ cup /50 g	⅝ cup /70 g	⅔ cup /75 g
Salmon oil	¼ tsp	½ tsp	½ tsp
Flaxseed (linseed) oil	1 tsp	Generous 1 tsp	1¼ tsp
Supplement	2⅓ tsp /6 g	Generous 3 tsp/8 g	3½ tsp /9 g

NUTRITION PER 3 ½ OZ/100 G

MACRONUTRIENTS

■ MINERALS ■ PROTEINS ■ FIBER
■ FATS ■ CARBOHYDRATES

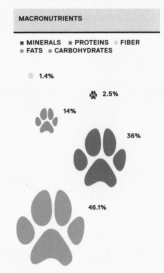

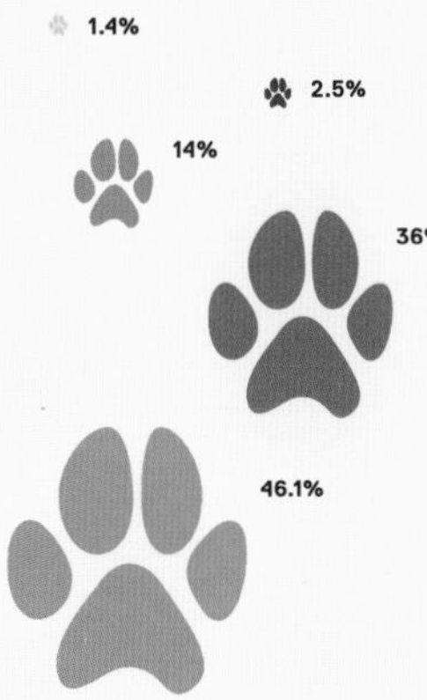
1.4%
2.5%
14%
36%
46.1%

DAILY QUANTITY

INGREDIENTS	ADULT WEIGHT: 6 LB 10 OZ/3 KG		
Dog Weight	1 lb 1 oz /0.5 kg	2 lb 2 oz /1 kg	4 lb 4 oz /2 kg
Beef	1½ oz /45 g	2½ oz /70 g	3¾ oz /105 g
White rice	4 tsp /15 g	2 tbsp /20 g	7 tsp /25 g
Spleen	⅓ oz /10 g	½ oz /15 g	½ oz /15 g
Carrots, sliced	4 tsp /10 g	1½ tbsp /15 g	1½ tbsp /15 g
Salmon oil	¼ tsp /1 g	¼ tsp /1 g	¼ tsp /1 g
Linseed oil	¼ tsp /1 g	¼ tsp /2 g	¼ tsp /2 g
Supplement	Generous tsp/3 g	1⅓ tsp /4 g	1⅓ tsp /4 g

NUTRITION PER 3 ½ OZ/100 G

MACRONUTRIENTS

■ MINERALS ■ PROTEINS ■ FIBER
■ FATS ■ CARBOHYDRATES

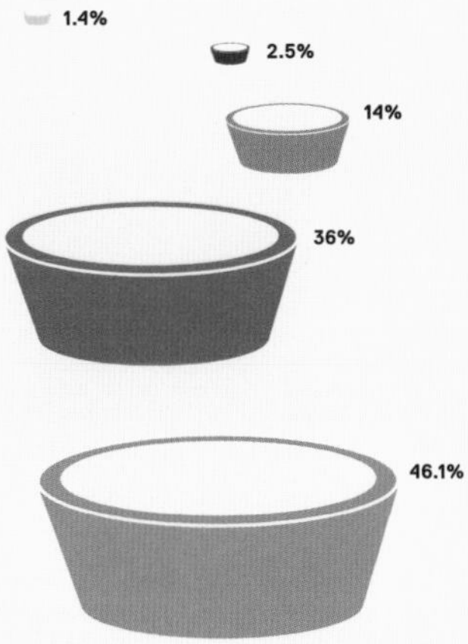
1.4%
2.5%
14%
36%
46.1%

Pasta with Carrot Sauce and Chicken

DAILY QUANTITY

INGREDIENTS	ADULT WEIGHT: 88 LB/40 KG					
Dog Weight	11 lb /5 kg	22 lb /10 kg	33 lb /15 kg	44 lb /20 kg	66 lb /30 kg	77 lb /35 kg
Chicken	7 oz /200 g	11 oz /310 g	13½ oz /385 g	15½ oz /440 g	1 lb 4¾ oz /590 g	1 lb 2½ oz /525 g
Durum wheat semolina pasta	3⅜ oz /95 g	5¼ oz /150 g	6⅜ oz /180 g	7⅜ oz /210 g	9⅜ oz /280 g	8¾ oz /250 g
Chicken liver	1¾ oz /50 g	2⅞ oz /80 g	3⅜ oz /95 g	3⅞ oz /110 g	5⅛ oz /145 g	4½ oz /130 g
Carrots, chopped	⅓ cup /50 g	¼ cup /35 g	½ cup /70 g	½ cup /70 g	1⅛ cup /145 g	1 cup /130 g
Salmon oil	½ tsp	⅔ tsp	⅞ tsp	1¼ tsp	1⅓ tsp	1⅓ tsp
Flaxseed (linseed) oil	2⅓ tsp	3⅔ tsp	4½ tsp	5¼ tsp	2¼ tbsp	2 tbsp
Supplement	1 tbsp + 1 tsp/10 g	2 tbsp + ⅓ tsp/16 g	2 tbsp + 2½ tsp /19 g	3 tbsp + ⅓ tsp /22 g	Scant 4 tbsp/29 g	3½ tbsp /26 g

NUTRITION PER 3½ OZ/100 G

MACRONUTRIENTS

■ MINERALS ■ PROTEINS ■ FIBER
■ FATS ■ CARBOHYDRATES

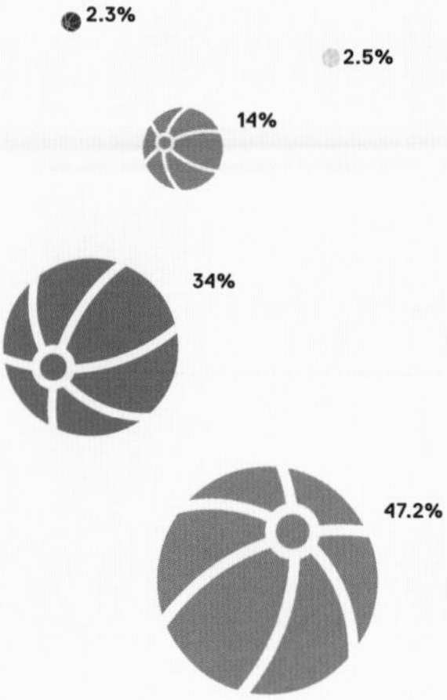

2.3%
2.5%
14%
34%
47.2%

DAILY QUANTITY

INGREDIENTS	ADULT WEIGHT: 55 LB/25 KG			
Dog Weight	11 lb /5 kg	22 lb /10 kg	33 lb /15 kg	44 lb /20 kg
Chicken	7 oz /200 g	9⅞ oz /280 g	12⅜ oz /350 g	12⅛ oz /345 g
Durum wheat semolina pasta	3⅜ oz /95 g	4¾ oz /135 g	5⅞ oz /165 g	5⅝ oz /160 g
Chicken liver	1¾ oz /50 g	2½ oz /70 g	3 oz /85 g	3 oz /85 g
Carrots, chopped	⅓ cup /50 g	½ cup /70 g	⅔ cup /85 g	⅔ cup /85 g
Salmon oil	½ tsp	⅔ tsp	⅞ tsp	⅞ tsp
Flaxseed (linseed) oil	2⅓ tsp	1 tbsp	4 tsp	4 tsp
Supplement	1 tbsp + 1 tsp/10 g	2 scant tbsp/14 g	2¼ tbsp/17 g	2¼ tbsp/17 g

NUTRITION PER 3½ OZ/100 G

MACRONUTRIENTS

■ MINERALS ■ PROTEINS ■ FIBER
■ FATS ■ CARBOHYDRATES

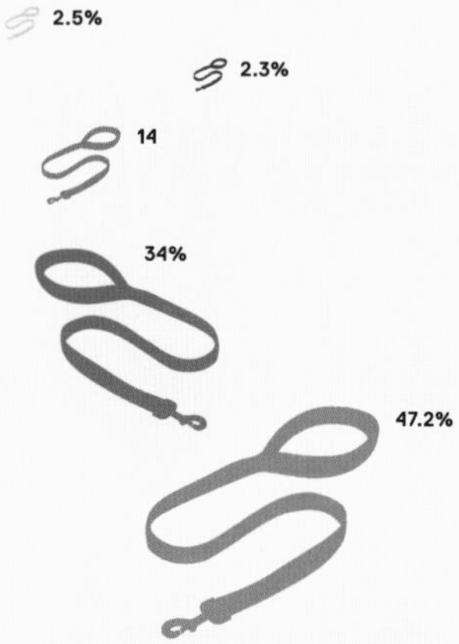

2.5%
2.3%
14
34%
47.2%

DAILY QUANTITY

INGREDIENTS	ADULT WEIGHT: 22 LB/10 KG		
Dog Weight	6 lb 6 oz /3 kg	13 lb 2 oz /6 kg	20 lb /9 kg
Chicken	4¼ oz /120 g	6 oz /170 g	6⅜ oz /180 g
Durum wheat semolina pasta	1½ oz /45 g	2¼ oz /65 g	2½ oz /70 g
Chicken liver	1¾ oz /50 g	2½ oz /70 g	2⅝ oz /75 g
Carrots, chopped	3½ tbsp /30 g	¼ cup /40 g	⅓ cup /45 g
Salmon oil	½ tsp	⅔ tsp	⅔ tsp
Flaxseed (linseed) oil	1¾ tsp	2⅓ tsp	2⅔ tsp
Supplement	Scant tbsp /7 g	1 tbsp + 1 tsp/10 g	1 tbsp + 1⅓ tsp/11 g

NUTRITION PER 3½ OZ/100 G

MACRONUTRIENTS

■ MINERALS ■ PROTEINS ▫ FIBER
■ FATS ■ CARBOHYDRATES

2.3%
2.5%
14%
34%
47.2%

DAILY QUANTITY

INGREDIENTS	ADULT WEIGHT: 6 LB 10 OZ/3 KG		
Dog Weight	1 lb 1 oz /0.5 kg	2 lb 2 oz /1 kg	4 lb 4 oz /2 kg
Chicken	1¼ oz /35 g	2 oz /55 g	2⅞ oz /80 g
Durum wheat semolina pasta	½ oz /15 g	¾ oz /20 g	⅞ oz /25 g
Chicken liver	⅓ oz /10 g	½ oz /15 g	⅞ oz /25 g
Carrots, chopped	1½ tbsp /15 g	5 tsp /20 g	3 tbsp /35 g
Salmon oil	¼ tsp	¼ tsp	½ tsp
Flaxseed (linseed) oil	¼ tbsp	½ tbsp	⅔ tbsp
Supplement	Scant tsp /2 g	Generous tsp/3 g	2 tsp /5 g

NUTRITION PER 3½ OZ/100 G

MACRONUTRIENTS

■ MINERALS ■ PROTEINS ▫ FIBER
■ FATS ■ CARBOHYDRATES

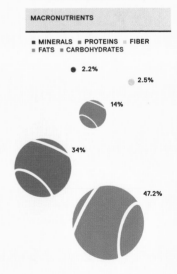

2.2%
2.5%
14%
34%
47.2%

Meaty Rice Timbale with Pumpkin

DAILY QUANTITY

INGREDIENTS	ADULT WEIGHT: 88 LB/40 KG					
Dog Weight	11 lb /5 kg	22 lb /10 kg	33 lb /15 kg	44 lb /20 kg	66 lb /30 kg	77 lb /35 kg
Pork	5¼ oz /150 g	8¼ oz /235 g	10 oz /285 g	11⅝ oz /330 g	15½ oz /440 g	13⅞ oz /395 g
Pig's spleen	3 oz /85 g	4¾ oz /135 g	5⅞ oz /165 g	6½ oz /185 g	8¾ oz /250 g	8 oz /225 g
Pig's heart	3 oz /85 g	4¾ oz /135 g	5⅞ oz /165 g	6½ oz /185 g	8¾ oz /250 g	8 oz /225 g
White rice	⅓ cup /65 g	½ cup /100 g	⅔ cup /125 g	¾ cup /145 g	1 cup /190 g	⅞ cup /170 g
Pumpkin or other winter squash, diced	⅓ cup /40 g	½ cup /60 g	⅔ cup /75 g	¾ cup /90 g	1 cup /120 g	⅞ cup /105 g
Flaxseed (linseed) oil	1½ tsp	2 tsp	2½ tsp	1 tbsp	4⅓ tsp	3⅔ tsp
Salmon oil	¼ tsp	½ tsp	⅔ tsp	⅔ tsp	⅞ tsp	⅞ tsp
Supplement	1 tbsp + 1 tsp/10 g	2 tbsp /16 g	2 tbsp + 2½ tsp/ 19 g	3 tbsp + ⅓ tsp/ 22 g	Scant 4 tbsp/29 g	3½ tbsp /26 g

NUTRITION PER 3½ OZ/100 G

MACRONUTRIENTS

■ MINERALS ■ PROTEINS ■ FIBER
■ FATS ■ CARBOHYDRATES

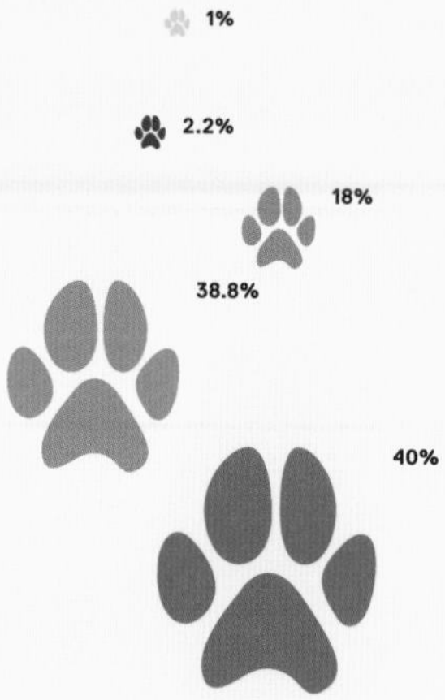

1%
2.2%
18%
38.8%
40%

DAILY QUANTITY

INGREDIENTS	ADULT WEIGHT: 55 LB/25 KG			
Dog Weight	11 lb /5 kg	22 lb /10 kg	33 lb /15 kg	44 lb /20 kg
Pork	5¼ oz /150 g	7⅜ oz /210 g	9⅛ oz /260 g	9 oz /255 g
Pig's spleen	3 oz /85 g	4¼ oz /120 g	5¼ oz /150 g	5⅛ oz /145 g
Pig's heart	3 oz /85 g	4¼ oz /120 g	5¼ oz /150 g	5⅛ oz /145 g
White rice	⅓ cup /65 g	½ cup /90 g	⅔ cup /115 g	⅝ cup /110 g
Pumpkin or other winter squash, diced	⅓ cup /40 g	½ cup /55 g	⅔ cup /70 g	⅝ cup /65 g
Salmon oil	¼ tsp	½ tsp	½ tsp	⅔ tsp
Flaxseed (linseed) oil	1½ tsp	2 tsp	2⅔ tsp	2¼ tsp
Supplement	1 tbsp + 1 tsp/10 g	Scant 2 tbsp/14 g	2¼ tbsp /17 g	2 tbsp + ⅓ tsp/16 g

NUTRITION PER 3½ OZ/100 G

MACRONUTRIENTS

■ MINERALS ■ PROTEINS ■ FIBER
■ FATS ■ CARBOHYDRATES

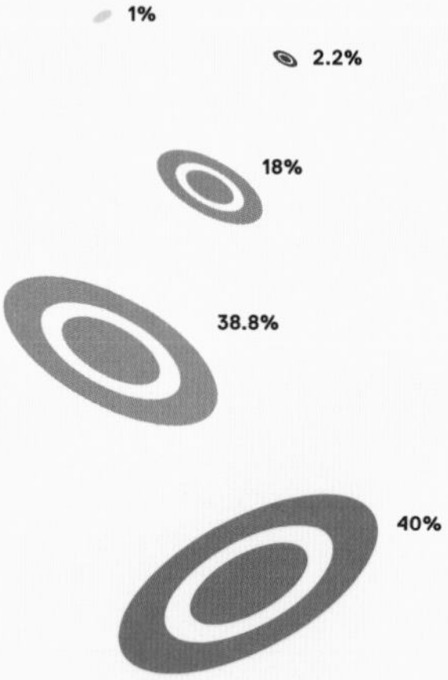

1%
2.2%
18%
38.8%
40%

DAILY QUANTITY

INGREDIENTS	ADULT WEIGHT: 22 LB/10 KG		
Dog Weight	6 lb 6 oz /3 kg	13 lb 2 oz /6 kg	20 lb /9 kg
Pork	3 oz /80 g	3⅞ oz /110 g	4¼ oz /120 g
Pig's spleen	1⅜ oz /40 g	2 oz /55 g	2⅛ oz /60 g
Pig's heart	2½ oz /70 g	3½ oz /100 g	3¾ oz /105 g
White rice	¼ cup /50 g	⅓ cup /70 g	⅜ cup /75 g
Pumpkin or other winter squash, diced	3 tbsp /20 g	¼ cup /30 g	⅓ cup /35 g
Salmon oil	¼ tsp	¼ tsp	½ tsp
Flaxseed (linseed) oil	½ tsp	⅞ tsp	⅞ tsp
Supplement	Scant tbsp /7 g	1 tbsp + 1 tsp /10 g	2 tbsp + 1⅓ tsp /11 g

NUTRITION PER 3½ OZ/100 G

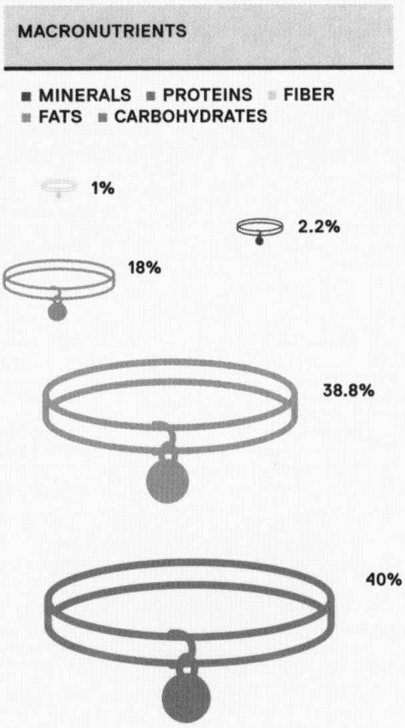
MACRONUTRIENTS
■ MINERALS ■ PROTEINS ■ FIBER
■ FATS ■ CARBOHYDRATES
1%
2.2%
18%
38.8%
40%

DAILY QUANTITY

INGREDIENTS	ADULT WEIGHT: 6 LB 10 OZ/3 KG		
Dog Weight	1 lb 1 oz /0.5 kg	2 lb 2 oz /1 kg	4 lb 4 oz /2 kg
Pork	1½ oz /20 g	2 oz /30 g	3 oz /55 g
Pig's spleen	¾ oz /10 g	1 oz /15 g	1½ oz /20 g
Pig's heart	1¼ oz /20 g	1½ oz /30 g	1½ oz /35 g
White rice	⅔ tbsp /10 g	1 tbsp /15 g	1 ⅓ tbsp /20 g
Pumpkin or other winter squash, diced	⅔ tbsp /10 g	1 tbsp /15 g	1 ⅔ tbsp /20 g
Salmon oil	¼ tsp	¼ tsp	⅓ tsp
Flaxseed (linseed) oil	¼ tsp	¼ tsp	⅓ tsp
Supplement	Scant tsp /2 g	Generous tsp/3 g	1⅔ tsp /4 g

NUTRITION PER 3½ OZ/100 G

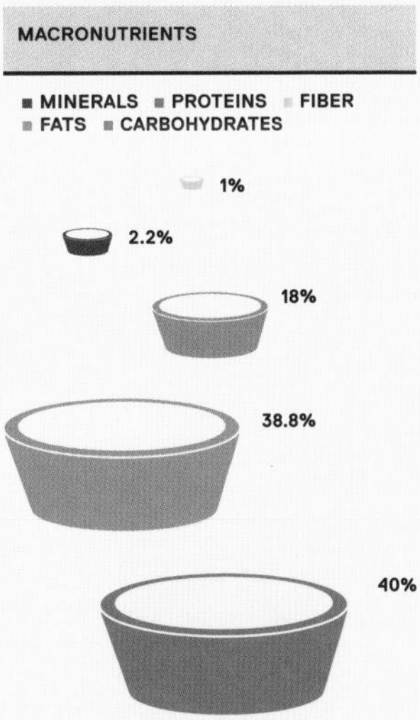
MACRONUTRIENTS
■ MINERALS ■ PROTEINS ■ FIBER
■ FATS ■ CARBOHYDRATES
1%
2.2%
18%
38.8%
40%

ADULT DOG NUTRITION

Pasta with Soybeans and Crispy Apple

P. 54

DAILY QUANTITY

INGREDIENTS	WEIGHT OF DOG					
Dog Weight	11 lb /5 kg	22 lb /10 kg	33 lb /15 kg	44 lb /20 kg	66 lb /30 kg	88 lb /40 kg
Canned soybeans	¼ cup /50 g	½ cup /85 g	⅔ cup /115 g	¾ cup /140 g	1 cup /190 g	1⅓ cups /240 g
Canned peas	2 tbsp /20 g	3½ tbsp /35 g	¼ cup /45 g	⅓ cup /55 g	½ cup /75 g	⅔ cup /95 g
Durum wheat semolina pasta	¾ oz /20 g	1¼ oz /35 g	1½ oz /45 g	2 oz /55 g	2⅝ oz /75 g	3⅜ oz /95 g
Sunflower oil	1 generous tsp	1 scant tbsp	1¼ tbsp	5 tsp	2 tbsp	2 tbsp, plus 2 tsp
Flaxseed (linseed) oil	½ tsp	1 tsp	1¼ tsp	2 tsp	1 tbsp	4 tsp
Brewer's dried yeast /or Marmite	1 scant tsp	1 tsp	2 tsp	1 tbsp	4 tsp	5 tsp
Apples, unpeeled, grated	2½ tbsp /30 g	¼ cup /50 g	⅓ cup /70 g	½ cup /85 g	⅔ cup /115 g	¾ cup /145 g
Vegan supplement	15 g	25 g	34 g	42 g	58 g	71 g
Supplement	2⅓ tsp /6 g	1 tbsp + 1 tsp/10g	2 tbsp/ 14 g	2⅔ tbsp /17 g	3 tbsp /23 g	3¾ tbsp /29 g

NUTRITION PER 3½ OZ/100 G

MACRONUTRIENTS

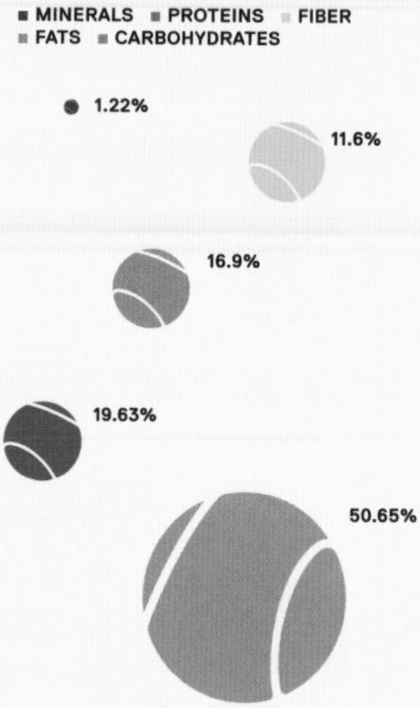
■ MINERALS ■ PROTEINS ■ FIBER
■ FATS ■ CARBOHYDRATES
1.22%
11.6%
16.9%
19.63%
50.65%

Vegetable and Cheese Rice Balls

P. 57

DAILY QUANTITY

INGREDIENTS	WEIGHT OF DOG					
Dog Weight	11 lb /5 kg	22 lb /10 kg	33 lb /15 kg	44 lb /20 kg	66 lb /30 kg	88 lb /40 kg
Canned soybeans	2½ tbsp /30 g	¼ cup /50 g	⅓ cup /70 g	½ cup /85 g	⅔ cup /115 g	¾ cup /145 g
Canned peas	3 tbsp /30 g	¼ cup /50 g	⅓ cup /70 g	½ cup /85 g	⅔ cup /115 g	¾ cup /145 g
Eggs	¼ cup /55 g	⅓ cup /90 g	½ cup /120 g	⅔ cup /150 g	⅞ cup /205 g	1 cup /250 g
White rice	2½ tbsp /30 g	¼ cup /50 g	⅓ cup /70 g	½ cup /85 g	⅔ cup /115 g	¾ cup /145 g
Sunflower oil	1 scant tsp	1 tsp	1½ tsp	2 tsp	1 tbsp	1½ tbsp
Cottage cheese	3 tbsp /40 g	¼ cup /65 g	⅜ cup /90 g	½ cup /115 g	⅔ cup /155 g	⅞ cup /190 g
Supplement	1½ tsp /4 g	Scant tbsp/7 g	1 tbsp + ⅔ tsp/9 g	1½ tbsp/ 11 g	2 tbsp 15 g	2 tbsp + 1 tsp /19 g

NUTRITION PER 3½ OZ/100 G

MACRONUTRIENTS

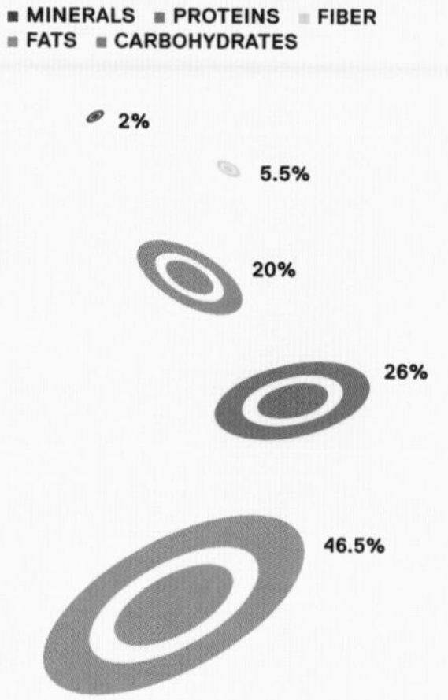
■ MINERALS ■ PROTEINS ■ FIBER
■ FATS ■ CARBOHYDRATES
2%
5.5%
20%
26%
46.5%

Pasta with Soy Meatballs and Eggs

P. 58

DAILY QUANTITY

INGREDIENTS	WEIGHT OF DOG					
Dog Weight	11 lb /5 kg	22 lb /10 kg	33 lb /15 kg	44 lb /20 kg	66 lb /30 kg	88 lb /40 kg
Canned soybeans	½ cup /80 g	¾ cup /135 g	1 cup /180 g	1¼ cups /225 g	1⅔ cups /305 g	2 cups /380 g
Sheep ricotta cheese	2½ tbsp /40 g	¼ cup /65 g	⅓ cup /90 g	½ cup /115 g	⅔ cup /155 g	¾ cup /190 g
Eggs	2 tbsp /25 g	3 tbsp /45 g	¼ cup /60 g	⅓ cup /75 g	⅓ cup + 1½ tbsp/ 105 g	½ cup /130 g
Durum wheat semolina pasta	¼ cup /30 g	scant ½ cup /50 g	scant ⅔ cup /70 g	¾ cup /85 g	1 cup /115 g	1¼ cups /145 g
Sunflower oil	½ tsp	½ tsp	1 scant tsp	1 tsp	1½ tsp	2 tsp
Supplement	2 tsp /5 g	Generous tbsp/8 g	1½ tbsp/ /11 g	Scant tbsp /14 g	2 tbsp + 1 tsp /19 g	3 tbsp + 1 tsp /24 g

NUTRITION PER 3½ OZ/100 G

MACRONUTRIENTS

■ MINERALS ■ PROTEINS ■ FIBER
■ FATS ■ CARBOHYDRATES

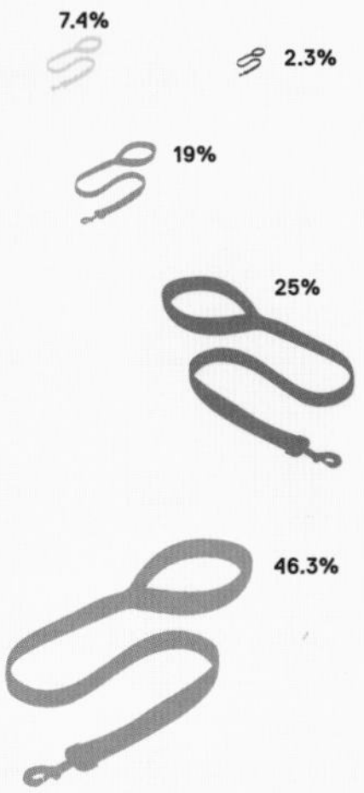
7.4%
2.3%
19%
25%
46.3%

Rice with Zucchini (Courgette)

P. 59

DAILY QUANTITY

INGREDIENTS	WEIGHT OF DOG					
Dog Weight	11 lb /5 kg	22 lb /10 kg	33 lb /15 kg	44 lb /20 kg	66 lb /30 kg	88 lb /40 kg
Chicken	2¼ oz /65 g	3⅞ oz /110 g	5¼ oz /150 g	6½ oz /185 g	9 oz /250 g	11 oz /310 g
Cod	2¼ oz /65 g	3⅞ oz /110 g	5¼ oz /150 g	6½ oz /185 g	9 oz /250 g	11 oz /310 g
Brown rice	¼ cup /45 g	⅓ cup /75 g	½ cup /105 g	⅓ cup /125 g	⅞ cup /175 g	1⅛ cups /215 g
Zucchini (courgette), sliced	¼ cup /80g	1⅓ cups /135 g	1⅔ cups /180 g	2 cups /225 g	2⅔ cups /305 g	3⅓ cups /380 g
Corn oil	½ tsp	1 tsp	1 tsp	1½ tsp	2 tsp	2½ tsp
Supplement	1½ tsp /4 g	Scant tbsp/7 g	1 tbsp + ⅔ tsp/9 g	1½ tbsp /11 g	2 tbsp /15 g	2 tbsp + 1 tsp/19 g

NUTRITION PER 3½ OZ/100 G

MACRONUTRIENTS

■ MINERALS ■ PROTEINS ■ FIBER
■ FATS ■ CARBOHYDRATES

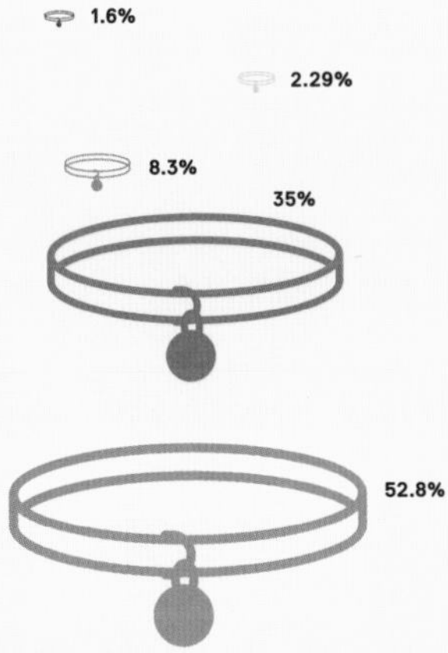
1.6%
2.29%
8.3%
35%
52.8%

Layered Rice, Fish, and Vegetables

P. 60

DAILY QUANTITY

INGREDIENTS	WEIGHT OF DOG					
Dog Weight	11 lb /5 kg	22 lb /10 kg	33 lb /15 kg	44 lb /20 kg	66 lb /30 kg	88 lb /40 kg
White rice	3 tbsp /35 g	⅓ cup /60 g	⅓ cup + 1½ tbsp /80 g	½ cup /100 g	¾ cup /135 g	⅞ cup /165 g
Hake	4⅜ oz /125g	7⅜ oz /210 g	10 oz /285 g	12½ oz /355 g	1 lb 1 oz /480 g	1 lb 5 oz /595 g
Green beans	⅓ cup /40 g	½ cup /65 g	¾ cup /90 g	1 cup /115 g	1⅓ cups /155 g	1¾ cups /190g
Corn oil	2 tsp	1 tbsp	4 tsp	5 tsp	6 ½ tsp	3 tbsp + 1 tsp
Supplement	1½ tsp /4 g	Scant tbsp /7 g	1 tbsp + ⅔ tsp/9 g	1½ tbsp /11 g	2 tbsp 15 g	2 tbsp + 1 tsp /19 g

NUTRITION PER 3½ OZ/100 G

MACRONUTRIENTS

■ MINERALS ■ PROTEINS ■ FIBER
■ FATS ■ CARBOHYDRATES

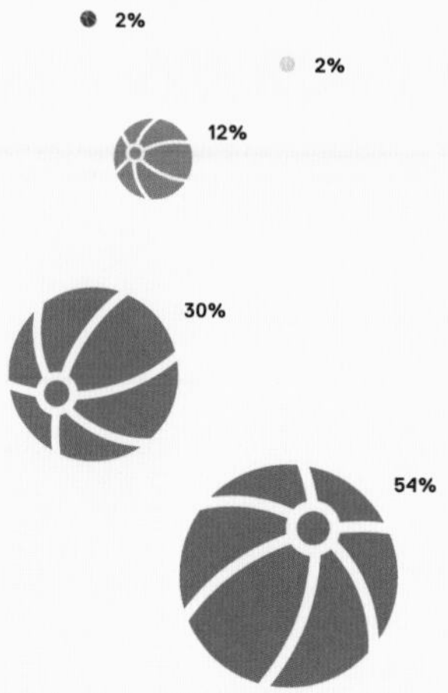
2%
2%
12%
30%
54%

Puffed Rice Patties

P. 62

DAILY QUANTITY

INGREDIENTS	WEIGHT OF DOG					
Dog Weight	11 lb /5 kg	22 lb /10 kg	33 lb /15 kg	44 lb /20 kg	66 lb /30 kg	88 lb /40 kg
Sardines	1 oz /30 g	1¾ oz /50 g	2½ oz /70 g	3 oz /85 g	4 oz /115 g	5⅛ oz /145 g
Veal	1¾ oz /50 g	3 oz /85 g	4 oz /115 g	5 oz /140 g	6¾ oz /190 g	8½ oz /240 g
Puffed rice	2 cups /30 g	3½ cups /50 g	5 cups /70 g	6 cups /85 g	8¼ cups /115 g	10⅓ cups /145 g
Green beans	⅓ cup /35 g	½ cup /60 g	¾ cup /80 g	⅞ cup /100 g	1¼ cups /135 g	1½ cups /165 g
Sunflower oil	2 tsp	1 tbsp	4 tsp	4½ tsp	2 tbsp	2 tbsp + 2 tsp
Supplement	1½ tsp /4 g	Scant tbsp/ 7 g	1 tbsp + ⅔ tsp/9 g	1½ tbsp /11 g	2 tbsp /15 g	2 tbsp + 1 tsp /19 g

NUTRITION PER 3½ OZ/100 G

MACRONUTRIENTS

■ MINERALS ■ PROTEINS ■ FIBER
■ FATS ■ CARBOHYDRATES

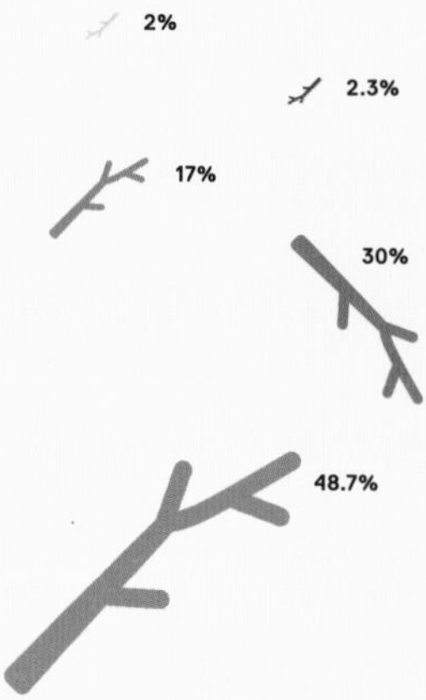
2%
2.3%
17%
30%
48.7%

Cod and Potato Casserole

P. 63

DAILY QUANTITY

INGREDIENTS	WEIGHT OF DOG					
Dog Weight	11 lb /5 kg	22 lb /10 kg	33 lb /15 kg	44 lb /20 kg	66 lb /30 kg	88 lb /40 kg
Cod	5¼ oz /150 g	8¾ oz /250 g	12 oz /340 g	14 oz /425 g	1 lb 4¼ oz /575 g	1 lb 9¼ oz /715 g
White potatoes, diced	⅓ cup /130 g	1½ cups /220 g	2 cups /295 g	2½ cups /370 g	3⅓ cups /500 g	4 cups /620 g
Sunflower oil	2 tsp	3½ tsp	5 tsp	6½ tsp	3 tbsp	3 tbsp + ½ tsp
Supplement	1½ tsp /4 g	Scant tbsp /7 g	1 tbsp + ⅔ tsp/9 g	1½ tbsp /11 g	2 tbsp /15 g	2 tbsp + 1 tsp /19 g

NUTRITION PER 3½ OZ/100 G

MACRONUTRIENTS

■ MINERALS ■ PROTEINS ■ FIBER
■ FATS ■ CARBOHYDRATES

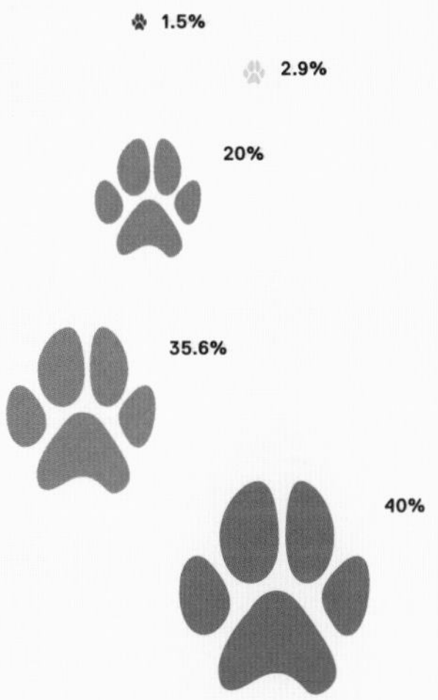
1.5%
2.9%
20%
35.6%
40%

Turkey and Rice Meatballs

P. 65

DAILY QUANTITY

INGREDIENTS	WEIGHT OF DOG					
Dog Weight	11 lb /5 kg	22 lb /10 kg	33 lb /15 kg	44 lb /20 kg	66 lb /30 kg	88 lb /40 kg
Skinless turkey breast	2⅞ oz /80 g	4¾ oz /135 g	6⅞ oz /180 g	8 oz /225 g	11 oz /310 g	13⅜ oz /380 g
White rice	3½ tbsp /40 g	⅓ cup /65 g	½ cup /90 g	⅔ cup /115 g	¾ cup /155 g	1 cup /190 g
Carrots, sliced	3 tbsp /20 g	¼ cup /35 g	⅜ cup /50 g	½ cup /55 g	⅔ cup /75 g	¾ cup /95 g
Zucchini (courgette), sliced	¼ cup /25 g	⅓ cup /40 g	½ cup /55 g	⅔ cup /70 g	¾ cup /90 g	1 cup /120 g
Sunflower oil	1 tsp	1½ tsp	2 tsp	2½ tsp	1 tbsp	4 tsp
Berries (blueberries, goji berries)	¾ tbsp /5 g	1½ tbsp /10 g	1½ tbsp /10 g	2 tbsp /15 g	2 tbsp /20 g	¼ cup /25 g
Supplement	1½ tsp /4 g	Scant tbsp /7 g	1 tbsp + ⅔ tsp/9 g	1½ tbsp /11 g	2 tbsp /15 g	2 tbsp + 1 tsp/19 g

NUTRITION PER 3½ OZ/100 G

MACRONUTRIENTS

■ MINERALS ■ PROTEINS ■ FIBER
■ FATS ■ CARBOHYDRATES

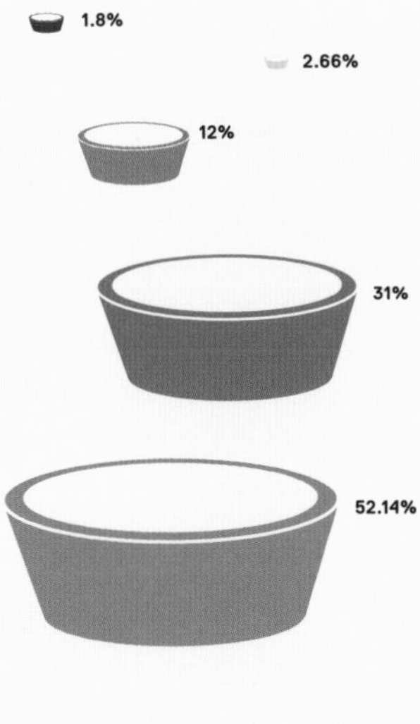
1.8%
2.66%
12%
31%
52.14%

Turkey and Ricotta Quenelles

P. 66

DAILY QUANTITY

INGREDIENTS	WEIGHT OF DOG					
Dog Weight	11 lb /5 kg	22 lb /10 kg	33 lb /15 kg	44 lb /20 kg	66 lb /30 kg	88 lb /40 kg
Skinless turkey breast	2¼ oz /60 g	3½ oz /100 g	4¾ oz /135 g	6 oz /170 g	8⅓ oz /230 g	10 oz /285 g
Ricotta	2½ tbsp /40 g	¼ cup /65 g	⅓ cup /90 g	½ cup /115 g	⅔ cup /155 g	¾ cup /190 g
Puffed rice	2 cups /30 g	3½ cups /50 g	5 cups /70 g	6 cups /85 g	8¼ cups /115 g	10½ cups /145 g
Carrots, grated	⅓ cup /40 g	½ cup /65 g	¾ cup /90 g	1 cup /115 g	1½ cups /155 g	1¾ cups /190 g
Sunflower oil	½ tsp	1 generous tsp	1¼ tsp	2 tsp	1 tbsp	4 tsp
Supplement	1½ tsp /4 g	Scant tbsp /7 g	1 tbsp + ⅔ tsp/9 g	1½ tbsp/ 11 g	2 tbsp /15 g	2 tbsp + 1 tsp/19 g

NUTRITION PER 3½ OZ/100 G

MACRONUTRIENTS

■ MINERALS ■ PROTEINS ▪ FIBER
■ FATS ■ CARBOHYDRATES

2.4%

2.4%

14%

28%

53.2%

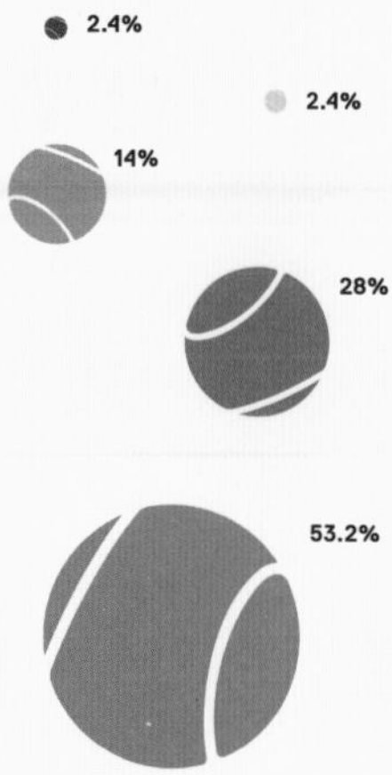

Oats, Turkey, and Potatoes

P. 67

DAILY QUANTITY

INGREDIENTS	WEIGHT OF DOG					
Dog Weight	11 lb /5 kg	22 lb /10 kg	33 lb /15 kg	44 lb /20 kg	66 lb /30 kg	88 lb /40 kg
Skinless turkey breast	3⅓ oz /90 g	5¼ oz /150 g	7¼ oz /205 g	9 oz /255 g	12⅓ oz /345 g	15¼ oz /430 g
Oat flakes	½ cup /25 g	¾ cup /40 g	1 cup /55 g	1⅓ cups /70 g	2 cups /95 g	2⅓ cups /120 g
Potatoes, peeled and diced	⅓ cup /50 g	⅔ cup /90 g	¾ cup /115 g	1 cup /140 g	1¼ cups /190 g	1⅔ cups /240 g
Kefir	2 tbsp /30 ml	2 tbsp + 2 tsp/35 ml	3 tbsp + 1 tsp/50 ml	¼ cup /75 ml	½ cup /115 ml	½ cup /140 ml
Sunflower oil	1 tsp	1½ tsp	1 tbsp	Scant 2 tbsp/14 g	3 ½ tsp	5 tsp
Supplement	2 tsp/5 g	Generous tbsp/8 g	1 tbsp + 1⅓ tsp /11 g	Scant 2 tbsp/14 g	2 tbsp + 1½ tsp /19 g	3¼ tbsp /24 g

NUTRITION PER 3½ OZ/100 G

MACRONUTRIENTS

■ MINERALS ■ PROTEINS ▪ FIBER
■ FATS ■ CARBOHYDRATES

2.6%

3.9%

15%

34%

44.5%

NUTRITIONAL VALUES

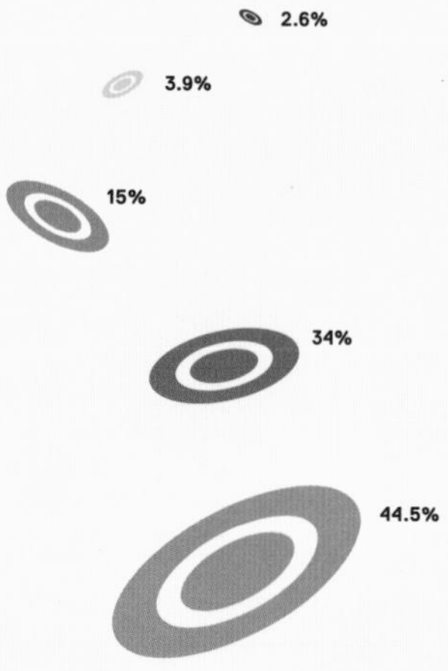

Cornmeal with Cheddar and Chicken

P. 69

DAILY QUANTITY

INGREDIENTS	WEIGHT OF DOG					
Dog Weight	11 lb /5 kg	22 lb /10 kg	33 lb /15 kg	44 lb /20 kg	66 lb /30 kg	88 lb /40 kg
Chicken breast or thigh	1 oz /30 g	1¾ oz /50 g	2½ oz /70 g	3 oz /85 g	4 oz /115 g	5⅛ oz /145 g
Chicken livers	¾ oz /20 g	1¼ oz /35 g	1½ oz /45 g	2 oz /55 g	2⅝ oz /75 g	3⅜ oz /95 g
Cornmeal (instant polenta)	3½ tbsp /30 g	⅓ cup /50 g	½ cup /70 g	⅔ cup /85 g	⅞ cup /115 g	1 cup /145 g
Squash, finely diced	2 tsp /30 g	1 tbsp /50 g	1¼ tbsp /70 g	1¼ tbsp /80 g	1½ tbsp /115 g	1½ tbsp /140 g
Sunflower oil	1½ tsp	2½ tsp	1 tbsp	4 tsp	5 tsp	2 tbsp
Cheddar cheese, grated	2 tbsp /30 g	3¼ tbsp /50 g	3½ tbsp/65 g	5½ tbsp /80 g	1⅓ cups /115 g	1⅔ cups 145 g
Supplement	2 tsp/5 g	Generous tbsp/8 g	1 tbsp + 1⅓ tsp /11 g	Scant 2 tbsp/14 g	2 tbsp + 1½ tsp /19 g	3¼ tbsp /24 g

NUTRITION PER 3½ OZ/100 G

MACRONUTRIENTS

■ MINERALS ■ PROTEINS ■ FIBER
■ FATS ■ CARBOHYDRATES

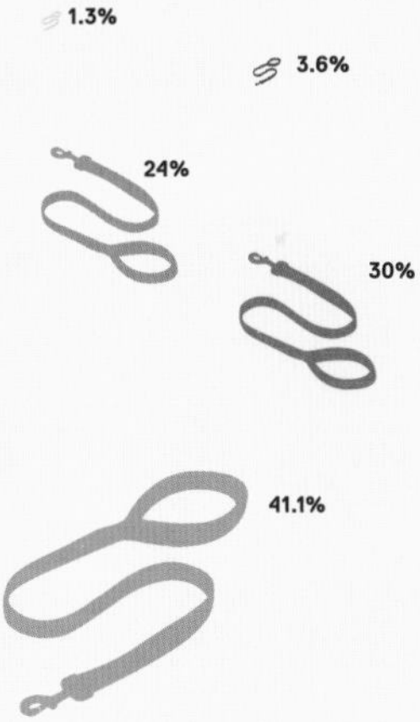
1.3%
3.6%
24%
30%
41.1%

Roman-Style Stuffed Rice Balls

P. 70

DAILY QUANTITY

INGREDIENTS	WEIGHT OF DOG					
Dog Weight	11 lb /5 kg	22 lb /10 kg	33 lb /15 kg	44 lb /20 kg	66 lb /30 kg	88 lb /40 kg
Chicken breast	2⅞ oz /80 g	4¾ oz /135 g	6⅜ oz /180 g	8 oz /225 g	10¾ oz /305 g	13⅜ oz /380 g
White rice	2½ tbsp /30 g	¼ cup /50 g	⅓ cup /70 g	½ cup /85 g	⅔ cup /115 g	¾ cup /145 g
Sunflower oil	1 tsp	1½ tsp	1¾ tsp	2 tsp	1 tbsp	3¾ tsp
Flaxseed (linseed) oil	1 tsp	1½ tsp	2 tsp	2¼ tsp	1 tbsp	4 tsp
Salmon oil	1 tsp	1½ tsp	2 tsp	2¼ tsp	1 tbsp	4 tsp
Apples, unpeeled, grated	⅓ cup /60 g	½ cup /100 g	¾ cup /135 g	⅞ cup /170 g	1¼ cups /230 g	1½ cups /285 g
Maltodextrin	2½ tsp /10 g	4¼ tsp /17 g	2 tbsp/ 23 g	2½ tbsp /28 g	3 tbsp /38 g	¼ cup /48 g
Parmesan cheese, grated	3 tbsp /20 g	5 tbsp /35 g	⅓ cup /45 g	½ cup /55 g	⅔ cup /75 g	¾ cup /95 g
Supplement	2⅓ tsp /6 g	1 tbsp + 1 tsp /10 g	Scant 2 tbsp /14 g	2¼ tbsp /17 g	3 tbsp /23 g	Scant 4 tbsp/29 g

NUTRITION PER 3½ OZ/100 G

MACRONUTRIENTS

■ MINERALS ■ PROTEINS ■ FIBER
■ FATS ■ CARBOHYDRATES

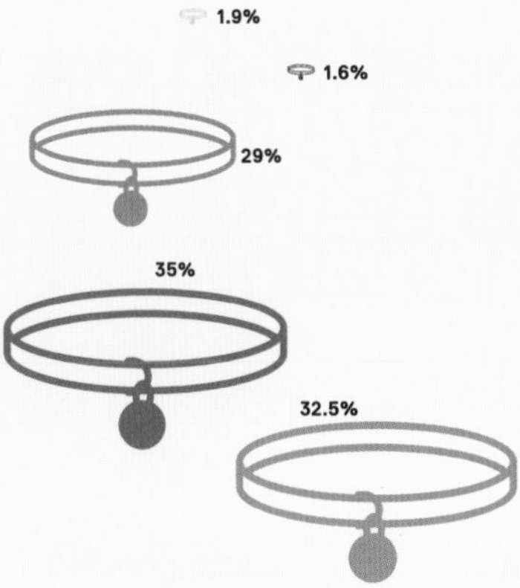
1.9%
1.6%
29%
35%
32.5%

Chicken and Apple Meatballs

P. 72

DAILY QUANTITY

INGREDIENTS	WEIGHT OF DOG					
Dog Weight	11 lb /5 kg	22 lb /10 kg	33 lb /15 kg	44 lb /20 kg	66 lb /30 kg	88 lb /40 kg
Chicken breast or thigh	2⅞ oz /70 g	4¼ oz /120 g	5⅔ oz /160 g	7 oz /200 g	9½ oz /270 g	12 oz /340 g
White rice	⅓ cup /25 g	¼ cup /40 g	⅓ cup /55 g	½ cup /70 g	¾ cup /95 g	1 cup /120 g
Pumpkin	¼ cup /20 g	⅓ cup /35 g	⅞ cup /45 g	½ cup /55 g	¾ cup /75 g	Scant cup /95 g
Lard	¼ tsp /2 g	⅓ tsp /3 g	1 tsp /5 g	1¼ tsp /6 g	1½ tsp /8 g	2 tsp /10 g
Sunflower oil	1 scant tsp	1 tsp	2 tsp	2 tsp	1 tbsp	3½ tsp
Flaxseed (linseed) oil	1 scant tsp	1 tsp	2 tsp	2 tsp	1 tbsp	3½ tsp
Salmon oil	1 scant tsp	1 tsp	2 tsp	2 tsp	1 tbsp	3½ tsp
Apples, unpeeled, grated	1 tbsp /20 g	2 tbsp /35 g	⅞ cup /45 g	¼cup /55 g	⅔ cup /75 g	½ cup /95 g
Maltodextrin	4 tsp	2 tbsp	3 tbsp	¼ cup /25 g	5 tbsp	6 tbsp
Parmesan cheese, grated	1 tbsp /5 g	4½ tbsp/8 g	10 tbsp /11 g	½ cup /15 g	⅔ cup /20 g	¾ cup /25 g
Supplement	1⅔ tsp/4 g	2¼ tsp /6 g	1 tbsp + 1⅓ tsp /9 g	1 tbsp + 1½ tsp/11 g	2 tbsp /15 g	2½ tbsp /20 g

NUTRITION PER 3½ OZ/100 G

MACRONUTRIENTS

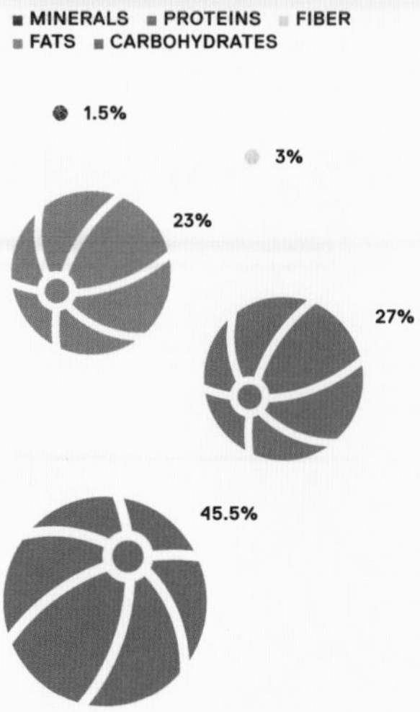

■ MINERALS ■ PROTEINS ■ FIBER
■ FATS ■ CARBOHYDRATES
1.5%
3%
23%
27%
45.5%

Soft-Boiled Egg with Squash and Chicken

P. 75

DAILY QUANTITY

INGREDIENTS	WEIGHT OF DOG					
Dog Weight	11 lb /5 kg	22 lb /10 kg	33 lb /15 kg	44 lb /20 kg	66 lb /30 kg	88 lb /40 kg
Chicken breast or thigh	2⅛ oz /60 g	3½ oz /100 g	4¾ oz /135 g	6 oz /170 g	8⅛ oz /230 g	10 oz /285 g
White rice	¼ cup /40 g	⅓ cup /65 g	½ cup /90 g	⅔ cup /115 g	¾ cup /155 g	1 cup /190 g
Eggs	1 tbsp /15 g	2 tbsp /25 g	2 tbsp /35 g	2½ tbsp /40 g	3½ tbsp /55 g	5 tbsp /70 g
Squash, finely chopped	1½ tbsp /30 g	2¼ tbsp /50 g	3½ tbsp /70 g	⅓ cup /85 g	⅜ cup /115 g	1 cup /145 g
Sunflower oil	2 tsp	3 tsp	1 tbsp	1 tbsp	4 tsp	4½ tsp
Salmon oil	¼ tsp	½ tsp	¾ tsp	1 tsp	1 tsp	1½ tsp
Supplement	1⅔ tsp /4 g	Scant tbsp /7 g	1 tbsp + ½ tsp/9 g	1 tbsp + 1⅓ tsp /11 g	2 tbsp /15 g	2 tbsp + 1½ tsp/ 19 g

NUTRITION PER 3½ OZ/100 G

MACRONUTRIENTS

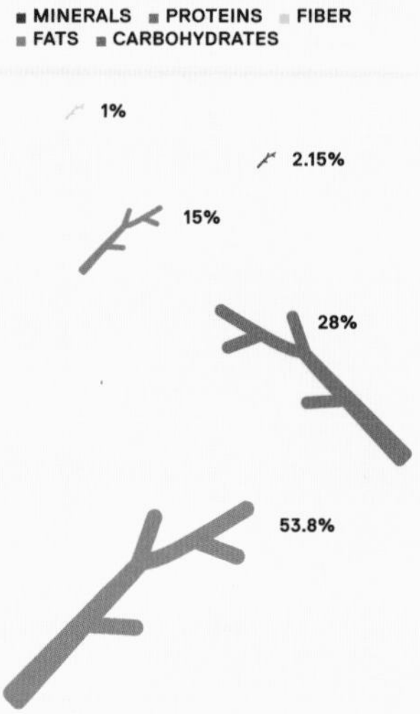

■ MINERALS ■ PROTEINS ■ FIBER
■ FATS ■ CARBOHYDRATES
1%
2.15%
15%
28%
53.8%

Chicken, Pork, and Vegetable Rice

P. 76

DAILY QUANTITY

INGREDIENTS	WEIGHT OF DOG					
Dog Weight	11 lb /5 kg	22 lb /10 kg	33 lb /15 kg	44 lb /20 kg	66 lb /30 kg	88 lb /40 kg
Pork neck or shoulder	3⅛ oz /90 g	5½ oz /155 g	7¼ oz /205 g	9 oz /255 g	12⅛ oz /345 g	15⅛ oz /430 g
White rice	1½ tbsp /20 g	3 tbsp /35 g	¼ cup /45 g	⅓ cup /55 g	⅜ cup /75 g	½ cup /95 g
Chicken giblets	1 oz /30 g	1¾ oz /50 g	2½ oz /70 g	3 oz /85 g	4 oz /115 g	5⅛ oz /145 g
Green beans, finely chopped	¼ cup /30 g	½ cup /50 g	⅔ cup /70 g	¾ cup /85 g	1 cup /115 g	1¼ cups /145 g
Carrots, sliced	¼ cup /30 g	⅓ cup /50 g	½ cup /70 g	¾ cup /85 g	1 cup /115 g	generous ¾ cup /145 g
Sunflower oil	1 scant tsp	1 generous tsp	2 scant tsp	2 generous tsp	1 scant tbsp	1 tbsp
Supplement	Generous tsp/3 g	2 tsp/5 g	Scant tbsp /7 g	Generous tbsp/8 g	1 tbsp + 2 tsp/12 g	Scant 2 tbsp/14 g

NUTRITION PER 3½ OZ/100 G

MACRONUTRIENTS

■ MINERALS ■ PROTEINS ■ FIBER
■ FATS ■ CARBOHYDRATES

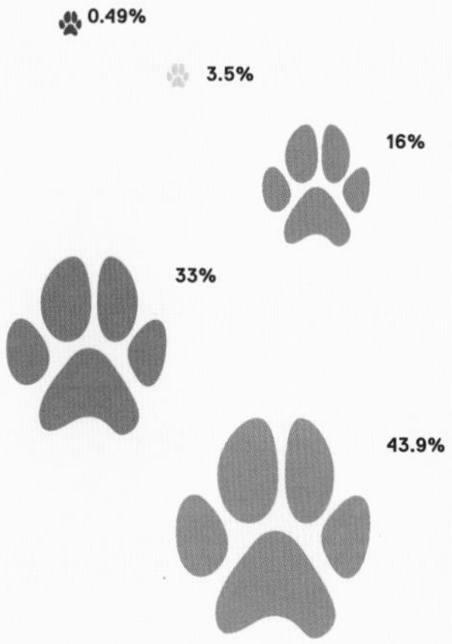
0.49%
3.5%
16%
33%
43.9%

Duck and Quinoa Salad

P. 77

DAILY QUANTITY

INGREDIENTS	WEIGHT OF DOG					
Dog Weight	11 lb /5 kg	22 lb /10 kg	33 lb /15 kg	44 lb /20 kg	66 lb /30 kg	88 lb /40 kg
Duck, skin on	1¾ oz /50 g	3 oz /85 g	4 oz /115 g	5 oz /140 g	6¾ oz /190 g	8½ oz /240g
Quinoa	4 tbsp /40 g	6½ tbsp /65 g	⅔ cup /90 g	¾ cup /115 g	Generous cup /155 g	1½ cups /190 g
Flaxseed (linseed) oil	1 scant tsp	1 tsp	1½ tsp	2 tsp	1 tbsp	3½ tsp
Sunflower oil	1 scant tsp	1 tsp	1½ tsp	2 tsp	1 tbsp	3½ tsp
Extra-virgin olive oil	1 scant tsp	1 tsp	1½ tsp	2 tsp	1 tbsp	3½ tsp
Zucchini (courgette), julienned	3 tbsp /30 g	5 tbsp /50 g	½ cup /70 g	⅔ cup /85 g	¾ cup /115 g	Generous cup /145 g
Carrots, julienned	3 tbsp /30 g	5 tbsp /50 g	½ cup /70 g	⅔ cup /85 g	¾ cup /115 g	Generous cup /145 g
Supplement	2 tsp/5 g	Generous tbsp/8 g	1 tbsp + 1⅓ tsp /11 g	Scant 2 tbsp/14 g	2 tbsp + 1½ tsp /19 g	3¼ tbsp /24 g

NUTRITION PER 3½ OZ/100 G

MACRONUTRIENTS

■ MINERALS ■ PROTEINS ■ FIBER
■ FATS ■ CARBOHYDRATES

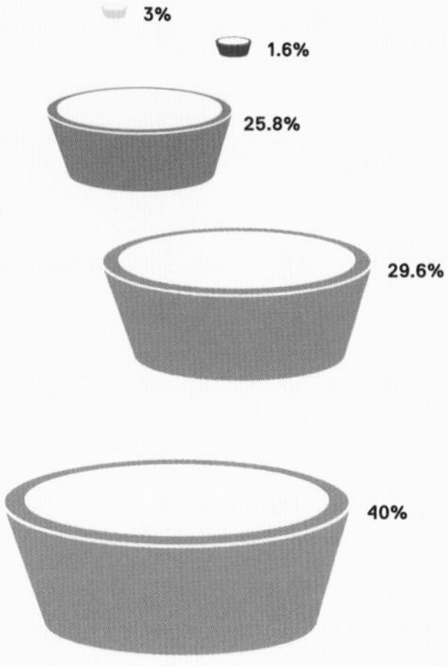
3%
1.6%
25.8%
29.6%
40%

Rabbit Stew with Potatoes and Kefir

P. 78

DAILY QUANTITY

INGREDIENTS	WEIGHT OF DOG					
Dog Weight	11 lb /5 kg	22 lb /10 kg	33 lb /15 kg	44 lb /20 kg	66 lb /30 kg	88 lb /40 kg
Rabbit thigh	⅞ oz /110 g	6½ oz /185 g	8¾ oz /250 g	11 oz /310 g	14¾ oz /420 g	1 lb 2½ oz /525 g
White potatoes, diced	¾ cup /110 g	1¼ cups /185 g	1⅔ cups /250 g	2 cups /310 g	2¾ cups /420 g	3½ cups /525 g
Kefir	4 tsp /40 ml	2 tbsp /65 ml	8 tsp /90 ml	½ cup /115 ml	⅔ cup /155 ml	¾ cup /190 ml
Corn oil	1 tsp	1 tbsp	1 tbsp	4 tsp	5 tsp	7 tsp
Supplement	1⅔ tsp /4 g	Scant tbsp /7 g	1 tbsp + ½ tsp/9 g	1 tbsp + 1⅓ tsp /11 g	2 tbsp /15 g	2 tbsp + 1½ tsp /19 g

NUTRITION PER 3½ OZ/100 G

MACRONUTRIENTS

■ MINERALS ■ PROTEINS ■ FIBER
■ FATS ■ CARBOHYDRATES

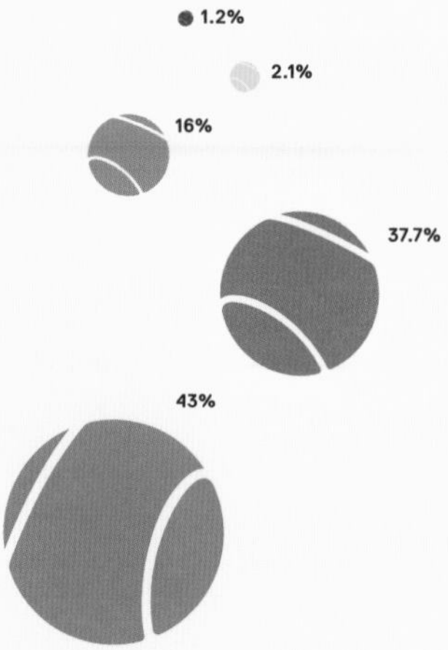
1.2%
2.1%
16%
37.7%
43%

Corn Pasta with Rabbit

P. 80

DAILY QUANTITY

INGREDIENTS	WEIGHT OF DOG					
Dog Weight	11 lb /5 kg	22 lb /10 kg	33 lb /15 kg	44 lb /20 kg	66 lb /30 kg	88 lb /40 kg
Rabbit thigh	2½ oz /70 g	3⅞ oz /110 g	5¼ oz /150 g	6½ oz /185 g	8¾ oz /250 g	11 oz /310 g
Corn pasta	1¼ oz /35 g	2⅛ oz /60 g	2⅞ oz /80 g	3½ oz /100 g	4¾ oz /135 g	5⅞ oz /165 g
Squash, peeled and diced	⅓ cup /40 g	½ cup /65 g	¾ cup /90 g	1 cup /115 g	1⅓ cups /155 g	1⅔ cups /190 g
Zucchini (courgette), diced	⅓ cup /40 g	½ cup /65 g	¾ cup /90 g	1 cup /115 g	1⅓ cups /155 g	1⅔ cups /190 g
Corn oil	1½ tsp	1 tbsp	4 tsp	5 tsp	7 tsp	3 tbsp
Supplement	1⅔ tsp /4 g	Scant tbsp/7 g	1 tbsp + ½ tsp/9 g	1 tbsp + 1⅓ tsp /11 g	2 tbsp /15 g	2 tbsp + 1½ tsp /19 g

NUTRITION PER 3½ OZ/100 G

MACRONUTRIENTS

■ MINERALS ■ PROTEINS ■ FIBER
■ FATS ■ CARBOHYDRATES

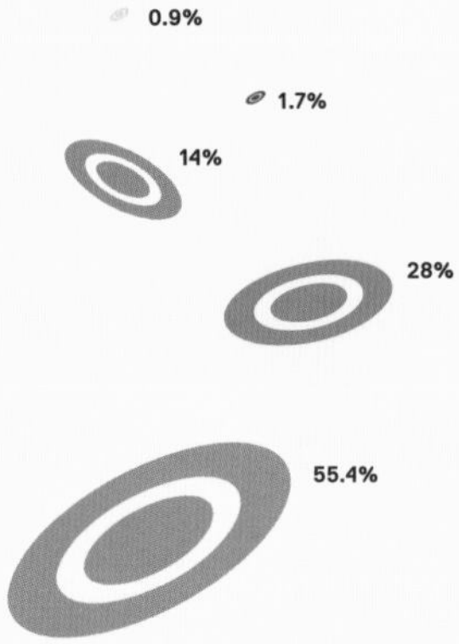
0.9%
1.7%
14%
28%
55.4%

Pork with Green Beans

P. 81

DAILY QUANTITY

INGREDIENTS	WEIGHT OF DOG					
Dog Weight	11 lb /5 kg	22 lb /10 kg	33 lb /15 kg	44 lb /20 kg	66 lb /30 kg	88 lb /40 kg
Pork neck or shoulder	3⅛ oz /90 g	5¼ oz /150 g	7¼ oz /205 g	9 oz /255 g	12⅛ oz /345 g	15⅛ oz /430 g
Pasta	1⅜ oz /40 g	2¼ oz /65 g	3⅛ oz /90 g	4 oz /115 g	5¼ oz /150 g	6¾ oz /190 g
Green beans	3 tbsp /35 g	3½ tbsp /60 g	¾ cup /80 g	1 cup /100 g	1¼ cups /135 g	1½ cups /165 g
Sunflower oil	½ tsp	¾ tsp	1 tsp	1¼ tsp	1½ tsp	2 tsp
Lard or suet	½ tsp	¾ tsp	1 tsp	2 tsp	2½ tsp	4 tsp
Dried rosemary	¼ tsp	¼ tsp	2 tsp	¾ tsp	1 tsp	1 tsp
Supplement	1⅔ tsp /4 g	Scant tbsp /7 g	1 tbsp + ½ tsp/9 g	1 tbsp + 1⅓ tsp /11 g	2 tbsp /15 g	2 tbsp + 1½ tsp /19 g

NUTRITION PER 3½ OZ/100 G

MACRONUTRIENTS

■ MINERALS ■ PROTEINS ■ FIBER
■ FATS ■ CARBOHYDRATES

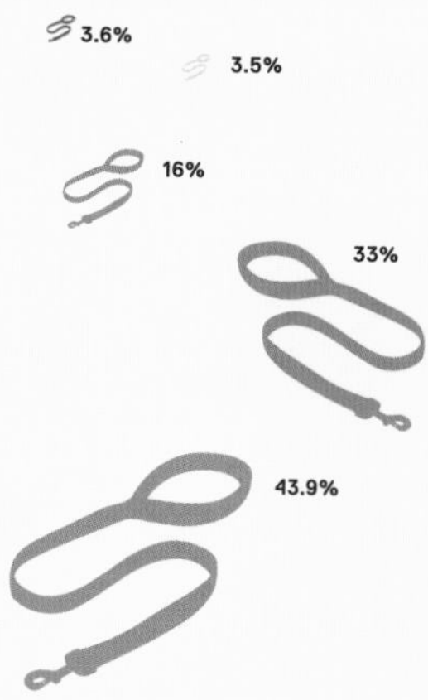
3.6%
3.5%
16%
33%
43.9%

Pasta Salad with Pork, Endives, and Yogurt

P. 82

DAILY QUANTITY

INGREDIENTS	WEIGHT OF DOG					
Dog Weight	11 lb /5 kg	22 lb /10 kg	33 lb /15 kg	44 lb /20 kg	66 lb /30 kg	88 lb /40 kg
Pork neck or shoulder	2½ oz /70 g	4¼ oz /120 g	5⅝ oz /160 g	7 oz /200 g	9½ oz /270 g	11⅝ oz /330 g
Whole milk (full fat) yogurt	2 tsp /30 ml	4 tsp /50 ml	2 tbsp /70 ml	3 tbsp + 2 tsp/85 ml	¼ cup /115 ml	5 tbsp /145 ml
Durum wheat semolina pasta	1 oz /35 g	2⅛ oz /60 g	2⅞ oz /80 g	3½ oz /100 g	4¾ oz /135 g	5⅞ oz /165 g
Endives	5 leaves /30 g	½ head /50 g	¾ head /70 g	1 head /85 g	1⅓ heads /115 g	1¾ heads /145 g
Sunflower oil	1 tsp	2 tsp	2½ tsp	1 tbsp	4 tsp	5 tsp
Supplement	1⅔ tsp /4 g	Scant tbsp/7 g	1 tbsp + ½ tsp/9 g	1 tbsp + 1⅓ tsp /11 g	2 tbsp /15 g	2 tbsp + 1½ tsp /19 g

NUTRITION PER 3½ OZ/100 G

MACRONUTRIENTS

■ MINERALS ■ PROTEINS ■ FIBER
■ FATS ■ CARBOHYDRATES

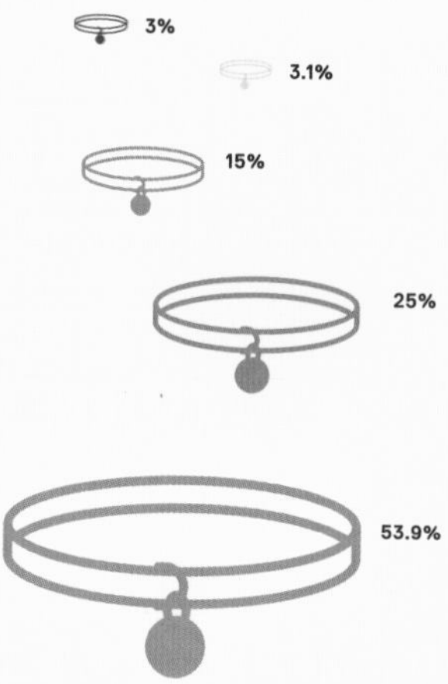
3%
3.1%
15%
25%
53.9%

Cornmeal with Surf and Turf

P. 83

DAILY QUANTITY

INGREDIENTS	WEIGHT OF DOG					
Dog Weight	11 lb /5 kg	22 lb /10 kg	33 lb /15 kg	44 lb /20 kg	66 lb /30 kg	88 lb /40 kg
Chicken breast	1¾ oz /50 g	3 oz /85 g	4 oz /115 g	5 oz /140 g	6¾ oz /190 g	8¼ oz /240 g
Hake	2⅞ oz /80 g	4¼ oz /135 g	6½ oz /185 g	8 oz /225 g	10¾ oz /305 g	13⅜ oz /380 g
Cornmeal (instant polenta)	¼ cup /40 g	½ cup /65 g	⅔ cups /90 g	⅞ cup /115 g	1⅛ cups /155 g	1⅓ cups /190 g
Sunflower oil	½ tsp	¾ tsp	1 tsp	1½ tsp	1 tbsp	1½ tbsp
Green beans	3 tbsp /20 g	⅓ cup /35 g	⅜ cup 45 g	½ cup /65 g	⅔ cup /75 g	¾ cup /95 g
Psyllium husks	¼ tsp	½ tsp	1 tsp	1 generous tsp	1¼ tsp	2 tbsp
Supplement	1⅔ tsp /4 g	Scant tbsp /7 g	1 tbsp + ½ tsp/9 g	1 tbsp + 1⅓ tsp /11 g	2 tbsp /15 g	2 tbsp + 1½ tsp /19 g

NUTRITION PER 3½ OZ/100 G

MACRONUTRIENTS

■ MINERALS ■ PROTEINS ■ FIBER
■ FATS ■ CARBOHYDRATES

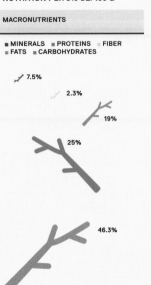

7.5%
2.3%
19%
25%
46.3%

Surf and Turf Rice and Potato Ring

P. 84

DAILY QUANTITY

INGREDIENTS	WEIGHT OF DOG					
Dog Weight	11 lb /5 kg	22 lb /10 kg	33 lb /15 kg	44 lb /20 kg	66 lb /30 kg	88 lb /40 kg
Lean veal	2⅛ oz /60 g	3½ oz /100 g	4¾ oz /135 g	6 oz /170 g	8⅛ oz /230 g	10 oz /285 g
White rice	2 tbsp /30 g	3 tbsp /50 g	⅓ cup /70 g	½ cup /85 g	⅔ cup /115 g	¾ cup /145 g
White potatoes, finely chopped	3 tbsp /30 g	½ cup /85 g	¾ cup /115 g	1 cup /140 g	1¼ cups /190 g	1⅔ cups /240 g
Cod	1⅜ oz /40 g	2¼ oz /65 g	3⅛ oz /90 g	4 oz /115 g	5½ oz /155 g	6¾ oz /190 g
Lard	1 tsp	2 tsp	1 tbsp	3½ tsp	4 tsp	2 tbsp
Corn oil	1 tsp	1½ tsp	2 tsp	2½ tsp	3½ tsp	4 tsp
Supplement	1⅔ tsp /4 g	Scant tbsp /7 g	1 tbsp + ½ tsp/9 g	1 tbsp + 1⅓ tsp /11 g	2 tbsp /15 g	2 tbsp + 1½ tsp /19 g

NUTRITION PER 3½ OZ/100 G

MACRONUTRIENTS

■ MINERALS ■ PROTEINS ■ FIBER
■ FATS ■ CARBOHYDRATES

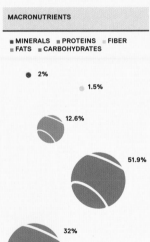

2%
1.5%
12.6%
51.9%
32%

NUTRITIONAL VALUES

Pasta with Zucchini (Courgette) and Lamb

P. 87

DAILY QUANTITY

INGREDIENTS	WEIGHT OF DOG					
Dog Weight	11 lb /5 kg	22 lb /10 kg	33 lb /15 kg	44 lb /20 kg	66 lb /30 kg	88 lb /40 kg
Lamb	2½ oz /70 g	4¼ oz /120 g	5⅝ oz /160 g	7 oz /200 g	9½ oz /270 g	11¾ oz /335 g
Durum wheat semolina pasta	1⅜ oz /40 g	2½ oz /70 g	3⅛ oz /90 g	4 oz /115 g	5½ oz /155 g	6¾ oz /190 g
Beef heart	⅞ oz /25 g	1⅜ oz /40 g	2⅛ oz /60 g	2½ oz /70 g	3⅜ oz /95 g	4¼ oz /120 g
Zucchini (courgette), sliced	⅓ cup /40 g	⅔ cup /70 g	¾ cup /90 g	1 cup /115 g	1⅓ cups /155 g	1⅔ cups /190 g
Sunflower oil	¼ tsp	½ tsp	⅔ tsp	¾ tsp	1 tsp	1½ tsp
Supplement	1⅔ tsp /4 g	Scant tbsp/7 g	1 tbsp + ½ tsp/9 g	1 tbsp + 1⅓ tsp /11 g	2 tbsp /15 g	2 tbsp + 1½ tsp /19 g

NUTRITION PER 3½ OZ/100 G

MACRONUTRIENTS

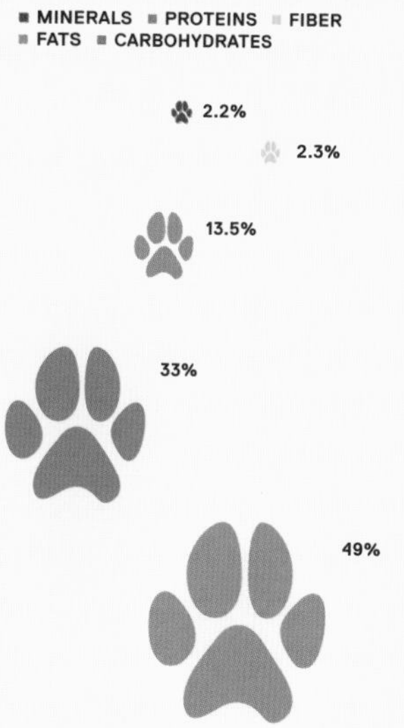

■ MINERALS ■ PROTEINS ■ FIBER
■ FATS ■ CARBOHYDRATES
2.2%
2.3%
13.5%
33%
49%

Couscous with Beef and Vegetables

P. 88

DAILY QUANTITY

INGREDIENTS	WEIGHT OF DOG					
Dog Weight	11 lb /5 kg	22 lb /10 kg	33 lb /15 kg	44 lb /20 kg	66 lb /30 kg	88 lb /40 kg
Lean beef	2⅞ oz /80 g	4¾ oz /135 g	6⅜ oz /180 g	8⅛ oz /230 g	11 oz /310 g	13⅜ oz /380g
Couscous	¼ cup /40 g	⅜ cup /70 g	½ cup /90 g	⅔ cup /110 g	⅞ cup /150 g	1⅛ cups /190 g
Peas	2 tbsp /20 g	3 tbsp /35 g	⅓ cup /50 g	½ cup /60 g	⅔ cup /80g	¾ cup /95 g
Carrots, grated	2½ tbsp/30 g	3 tbsp /50 g	5 tbsp /70 g	½ cup /85 g	⅔ cup /115 g	generous ¾ cup /145 g
Sunflower oil	1 tsp	1 tsp	2 tsp	2½ tsp	1 tbsp	3½ tsp
Supplement	1⅔ tsp /4 g	Scant tbsp/7 g	1 tbsp + ½ tsp /9 g	1 tbsp + 1⅓ tsp/11 g	2 tbsp /15 g	2 tbsp + 1½ tsp/19 g

NUTRITION PER 3½ OZ/100 G

MACRONUTRIENTS

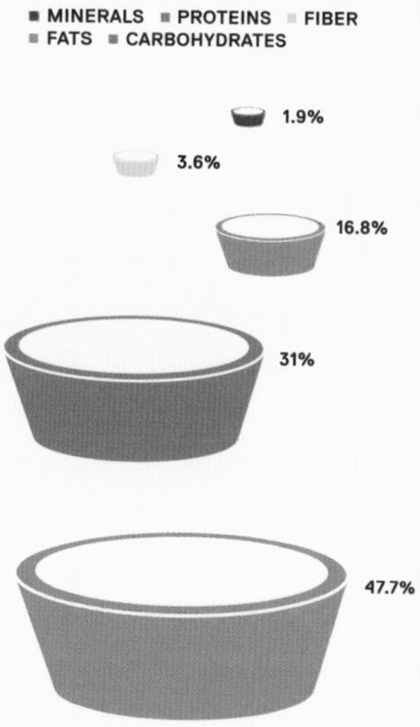

■ MINERALS ■ PROTEINS ■ FIBER
■ FATS ■ CARBOHYDRATES
1.9%
3.6%
16.8%
31%
47.7%

Buckwheat with Berries and Beef

P. 89

DAILY QUANTITY

INGREDIENTS	WEIGHT OF DOG					
Dog Weight	11 lb /5 kg	22 lb /10 kg	33 lb /15 kg	44 lb /20 kg	66 lb /30 kg	88 lb /40 kg
Lean beef	2⅛ oz /60 g	3½ oz /100 g	5 oz /140 g	6 oz /170 g	8⅛ oz /230 g	10 oz /285 g
Spleen	¾ oz /20 g	1¼ oz /35 g	1½ oz /45 g	2⅛ oz /60 g	2⅛ oz /80 g	3⅜ oz /95 g
Buckwheat	¼ cup /50 g	½ cup /85 g	⅔ cup /115 g	⅞ cup /140 g	1⅛ cups /190 g	1⅓ cups /240 g
Corn oil	1 tsp	2 tsp	2½ tsp	1 tbsp	4 tsp	1½ tbsp
Berries (blueberries, goji berries)	2 tsp /5 g	4 tsp /10 g	4 tsp /10 g	1 tbsp /15 g	1½ tbsp /20 g	1¾ tbsp /25 g
Supplement	2 tsp /5 g	Generous tbsp/8 g	1 tbsp+ 1⅓ tsp/11 g	Scant 2 tbsp/14 g	2 tbsp + 1½ tsp/19 g	3¼ tbsp/24 g

NUTRITION PER 3½ OZ/100 G

MACRONUTRIENTS

■ MINERALS ■ PROTEINS ■ FIBER
■ FATS ■ CARBOHYDRATES

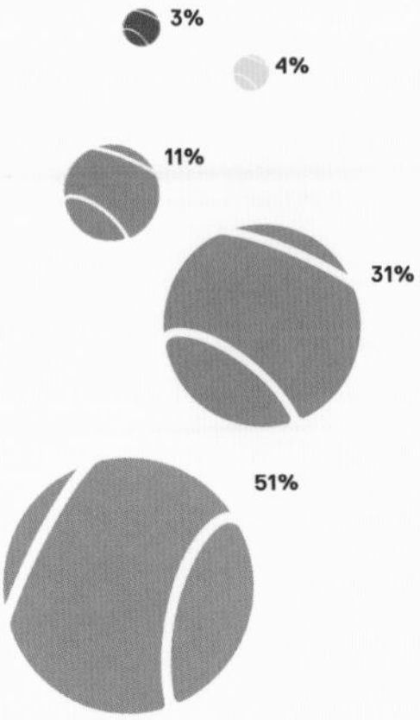
3%
4%
11%
31%
51%

Warm Buckwheat with Pork and Berries

P. 91

DAILY QUANTITY

INGREDIENTS	WEIGHT OF DOG					
Dog Weight	11 lb /5 kg	22 lb /10 kg	33 lb /15 kg	44 lb /20 kg	66 lb /30 kg	88 lb /40 kg
Buckwheat	3 tbsp /30 g	6 tbsp /50 g	⅜ cup /70 g	½ cup /85 g	⅔ cup /115 g	⅞ cup /145 g
Pork neck or shoulder	2½ oz /70 g	4¼ oz /120 g	5⅝ oz /160 g	7 oz /200 g	9½ oz /270 g	4⅝ oz /330 g
Pig's liver	¾ oz /20 g	1¼ oz /35 g	2⅛ oz /45 g	2⅝ oz /60 g	2½ oz /75 g	3⅜ oz /95 g
Corn oil	1 tsp	1½ tsp	2 tsp	1 tbsp	3½ tsp	4 tsp
Berries (blueberries, goji berries)	2 tsp /5g	1 tbsp /8 g	2 tbsp /11 g	2½ tbsp /14 g	3 tbsp /19 g	¼ cup /24 g
Supplement	12/3 tsp /4 g	Scant tbsp/7 g	1 tbsp + ½ tsp/9 g	1 tbsp+ 1⅓ tsp/11 g	2 tbsp /15 g	2 tbsp + 1½ tsp/19 g
Apple, grated	1½ tsp /5 g	¼ cup /45 g	¼ cup /45 g	⅓ cup /60 g	⅔ cup /115g	¾ cup /145 g

NUTRITION PER 3½ OZ/100 G

MACRONUTRIENTS

■ MINERALS ■ PROTEINS ■ FIBER
■ FATS ■ CARBOHYDRATES

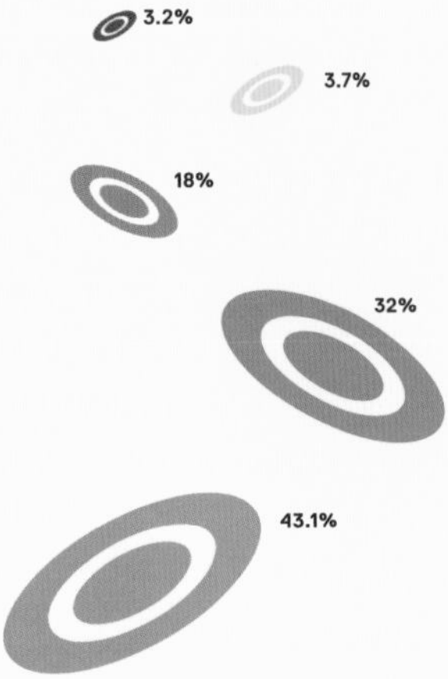
3.2%
3.7%
18%
32%
43.1%

Pork and Chicken Stew with Rice

P. 92

DAILY QUANTITY

INGREDIENTS	WEIGHT OF DOG					
Dog Weight	11 lb /5 kg	22 lb /10 kg	33 lb /15 kg	44 lb /20 kg	66 lb /30 kg	88 lb /40 kg
Rice	3 tbsp /30 g	¼ cup /50 g	⅓ cup /70 g	½ cup /85 g	⅔ cup /115 g	¾ cup /145 g
Carrots, cooked and pureed	3 tbsp /40 g	3½ tbsp /65 g	⅜ cup /90 g	½ cup /115 g	⅔ cup /155 g	⅞ cup /190 g
Extra-virgin olive oil	¼ tsp	¾ tsp	1 scant tsp	1 tsp	1½ tsp	2 tsp
Chicken livers	1⅜ oz /40 g	2¼ oz /65 g	3⅛ oz /90 g	4 oz /115 g	5½ oz /155 g	6 ¾ oz /190 g
Chicken breast or thigh	¾ oz /20 g	1¼ oz /35 g	2½ oz /45 g	2 oz /55 g	2½ oz /70 g	3⅜ oz /95 g
Pork neck or shoulder	1 oz /30 g	1 ¾ oz /50 g	2½ oz /70 g	3 oz /85 g	4 oz /115 g	5⅛ oz /145 g
Sunflower oil	¼ tsp	¾ tsp	1 scant tsp	1 tsp	1½ tsp	2 tsp
Supplement	1⅔ tsp /4 g	Scant tbsp/7 g	1 tbsp + ½ tsp/9 g	1 tbsp+ 1⅓ tsp/11 g	2 tbsp /15 g	2 tbsp + 1½ tsp/19 g

NUTRITION PER 3½ OZ/100 G

MACRONUTRIENTS

■ MINERALS ■ PROTEINS ■ FIBER
■ FATS ■ CARBOHYDRATES

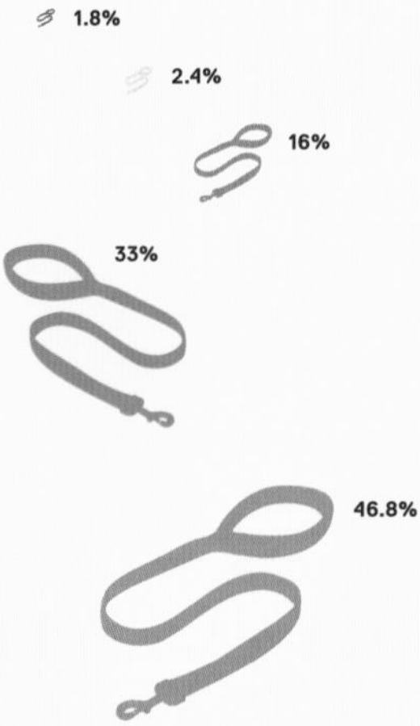
1.8%
2.4%
16%
33%
46.8%

Barley with Turkey, Beef, and Carrots

P. 93

DAILY QUANTITY

INGREDIENTS	WEIGHT OF DOG					
Dog Weight	11 lb /5 kg	22 lb /10 kg	33 lb /15 kg	44 lb /20 kg	66 lb /30 kg	88 lb /40 kg
Pearl barley	3 tbsp /35 g	⅓ cup /60 g	⅜ cup /80 g	½ cup /100 g	⅔ cup /135 g	⅞ cup /165 g
Beef tripe	⅞ oz /25 g	1⅜ oz /40 g	2 oz /55 g	2½ oz /70 g	3⅜ oz /95 g	4¼ oz /120 g
Turkey breast	1¾ oz /50 g	3 oz /85 g	4 oz /115 g	5 oz /140 g	6¾ oz /190 g	8½ oz /240 g
Carrots, grated	3 tbsp /20 g	⅓ cup /35 g	⅜ cup /45 g	½ cup /55 g	¾ cup /80 g	⅞ cup /95 g
Corn oil	2 tsp	1 tbsp	1 ½ tbsp	2 tsp	2¾ tbsp	3½ tbsp
Supplement	Generous tsp/3 g	2 tsp /5 g	Scant tbsp /7 g	Generous tbsp /8 g	1 tbsp + 1½ tsp /12 g	Scant 2 tbsp /14 g

NUTRITION PER 3½ OZ/100 G

MACRONUTRIENTS

■ MINERALS ■ PROTEINS ■ FIBER
■ FATS ■ CARBOHYDRATES

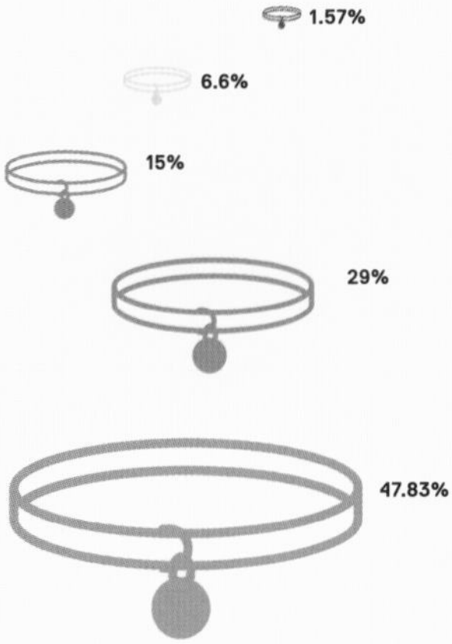
1.57%
6.6%
15%
29%
47.83%

Rice and Cheese Balls with Stew

P. 94

DAILY QUANTITY

INGREDIENTS	WEIGHT OF DOG					
Dog Weight	11 lb /5 kg	22 lb /10 kg	33 lb /15 kg	44 lb /20 kg	66 lb /30 kg	88 lb /40 kg
White rice	3 tbsp /30 g	5 tbsp /50 g	⅓ cup /70 g	½ cup /85 g	⅔ cup /125 g	¾ cup /145 g
Parmesan cheese, grated	6 tbsp /30 g	½ cup /50 g	¾ cup /70 g	⅞ cup /90 g	1 cup /115 g	1½ cups /145 g
Carrots, sliced	¼ cup /50 g	⅔ cup /85 g	½ cup /115 g	1¼ cup /140 g	1⅔ cups /190 g	2 cups /240 g
Lean veal	1⅜ oz /40 g	2½ oz /70 g	3⅛ oz /90 g	4 oz /115 g	3½ oz /155 g	6¾ oz /190 g
Sunflower oil	½ tsp	1 tsp	1½ tsp	2 tsp	2½ tsp	1 tbsp
Supplement	12/3 tsp /4 g	Scant tbsp/7 g	1 tbsp + ½ tsp/9 g	1 tbsp+ 1⅓ tsp/11 g	2 tbsp /15 g	2 tbsp + 1½ tsp/19 g

NUTRITION PER 3½ OZ/100 G

MACRONUTRIENTS

■ MINERALS ■ PROTEINS ■ FIBER
■ FATS ■ CARBOHYDRATES

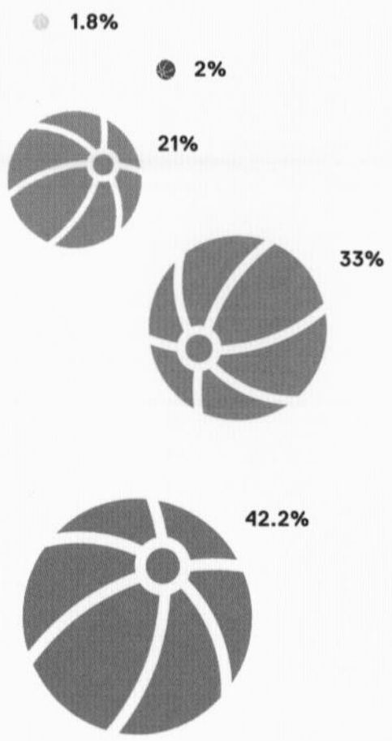

1.8%
2%
21%
33%
42.2%

Rosemary Cornmeal with Pork Meatballs

P. 95

DAILY QUANTITY

INGREDIENTS	WEIGHT OF DOG					
Dog Weight	11 lb /5 kg	22 lb /10 kg	33 lb /15 kg	44 lb /20 kg	66 lb /30 kg	88 lb /40 kg
Cornmeal (instant polenta)	¼ cup /40 g	½ cup /65 g	⅔ cup /85 g	¾ cup /110 g	1 cup /145 g	1⅓ cups /180 g
Ricotta	2 tbsp /30 g	3 tbsp /50 g	¼ cup /70 g	⅓ cup /85 g	½ cup /115 g	⅔ cup /145 g
Pork	2½ oz /70 g	4¼ oz /120 g	5⅝ oz /160 g	7 oz /200 g	9½ oz /270 g	11¾ oz /335 g
Zucchini (courgette), diced	¼ cup /30 g	⅓ cup /50 g	⅔ cup /70 g	¾ cup /85 g	1 cup /115 g	1¼ cups /145 g
Supplement	1⅔ tsp /4 g	Scant tbsp/7 g	1 tbsp + ½ tsp/9 g	1 tbsp+ 1⅓ tsp/11 g	2 tbsp /15 g	2 tbsp + 1½ tsp/19 g
Dried rosemary	1 tsp /2.5 g	1⅓ tsp /4 g	2⅓ tsp/6 g	1 tbsp /7.5 g	1 tbsp + ½ tsp /8.75 g	1 tbsp + 1 tsp /10 g
Supplement	1⅔ tsp /4 g	Scant tbsp/7 g	1 tbsp + ½ tsp/9 g	1 tbsp+ 1⅓ tsp/11 g	2 tbsp /15 g	2 tbsp + 1½ tsp/19 g

NUTRITION PER 3½ OZ/100 G

MACRONUTRIENTS

■ MINERALS ■ PROTEINS ■ FIBER
■ FATS ■ CARBOHYDRATES

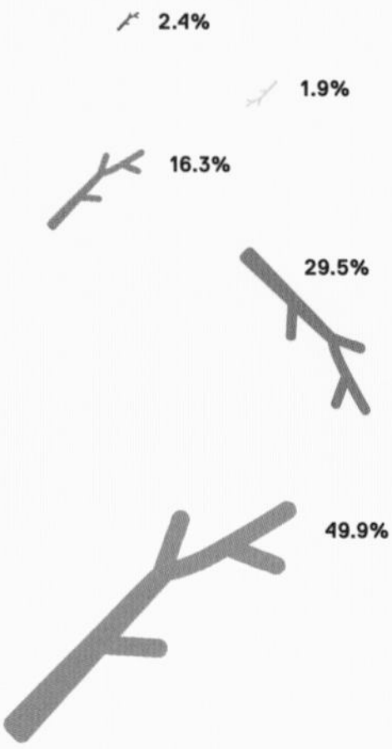

2.4%
1.9%
16.3%
29.5%
49.9%

Beef Roll and Potatoes

P. 96

DAILY QUANTITY

INGREDIENTS	WEIGHT OF DOG					
Dog Weight	11 lb /5 kg	22 lb /10 kg	33 lb /15 kg	44 lb /20 kg	66 lb /30 kg	88 lb /40 kg
Potatoes, diced	¾ cup /120 g	1⅓ cups /200 g	1¾ cups /275 g	2¼ cups /340 g	3 cups /460 g	4⅓ cups /570 g
Kefir	⅓ cup /80 ml	½ cup plus 1 tbsp /135 ml	¾ cup /180 ml	1 cup /225 ml	1⅓ cups /310 ml	1⅔ cups /380 ml
Lean veal	4¼ oz /120 g	7 oz /200 g	7¾ oz /275 g	10 oz /340 g	12 oz /460 g	1¼ lb /570 g
Linseed (flaxseed) oil	1 tsp	2 tsp	2½ tsp	3 tsp	1 tbsp	1⅓ tbsp
Supplement	1⅔ tsp /4 g	Scant tbsp/7 g	1 tbsp + ½ tsp/9 g	1 tbsp+ 1⅓ tsp/11 g	2 tbsp /15 g	2 tbsp + 1½ tsp/19 g

NUTRITION PER 3½ OZ/100 G

MACRONUTRIENTS

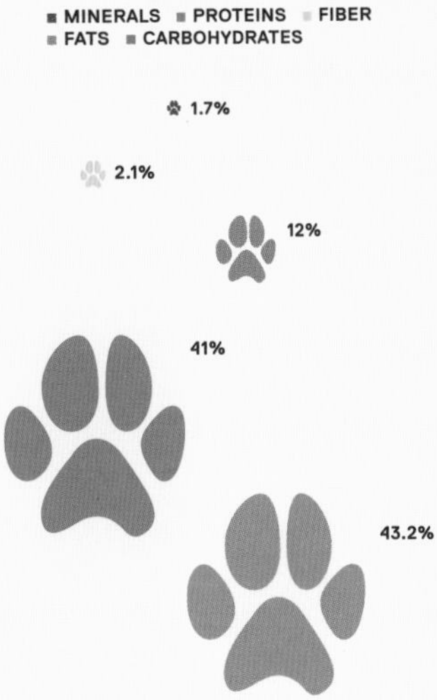
MINERALS
PROTEINS
FIBER
FATS
CARBOHYDRATES
1.7%
2.1%
12%
41%
43.2%

Pasta with Squash and Cornmeal

P. 98

DAILY QUANTITY

INGREDIENTS	WEIGHT OF DOG					
Dog Weight	11 lb /5 kg	22 lb /10 kg	33 lb /15 kg	44 lb /20 kg	66 lb /30 kg	88 lb /40 kg
Durum wheat semolina pasta	¾ oz /20 g	1¼ oz /35 g	1½ oz /45 g	2¼ oz /65 g	2⅝ oz /75 g	3⅜ oz /95 g
Squash, diced	⅓ cup /40 g	½ cup /65 g	⅔ cup /90 g	⅞ cup /115 g	1⅛ cups /155 g	1½ cups /190 g
Cornmeal (instant polenta)	1½ tbsp /13 g	¼ cup /35 g	⅓ cup /45 g	⅜ cup /55 g	½ cup /75 g	⅔ cup /95 g
Squash, diced	⅓ cup /40 g	½ cup /65 g	⅔ cup /90 g	⅞ cup /115 g	1⅛ cups /155 g	1½ cups /190 g
Veal	2¾ oz /80 g	4¾ oz /135 g	6½ oz /185 g	7⅞ oz /225 g	10¾ oz /305 g	13½ oz /380 g
Supplement	2⅓ tsp /6 g	1 tbsp + 1 tsp /10 g	Scant 2 tbsp /14 g	2 tbsp + ¾ tsp /17 g	3 tbsp /23 g	3⅞ tbsp /29 g
Corn oil	1 tsp	1 ¼ tsp	1½ tsp	2 tsp	1 tbsp	1 ½ tbsp

NUTRITION PER 3½ OZ/100 G

MACRONUTRIENTS

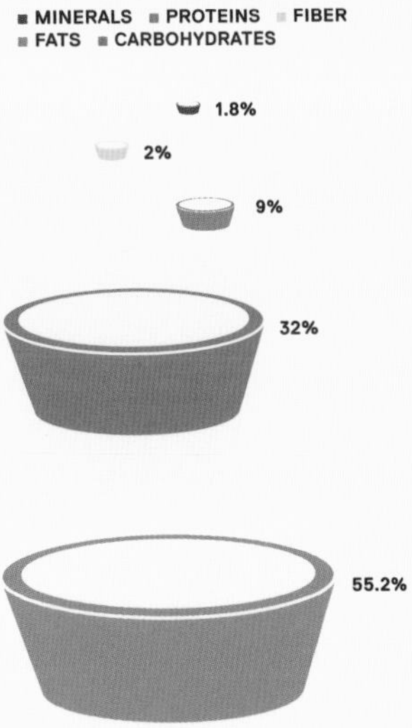
MINERALS
PROTEINS
FIBER
FATS
CARBOHYDRATES
1.8%
2%
9%
32%
55.2%

Beef Stew with Rice and Apple

P. 99

DAILY QUANTITY

INGREDIENTS	WEIGHT OF DOG					
Dog Weight	11 lb /5 kg	22 lb /10 kg	33 lb /15 kg	44 lb /20 kg	66 lb /30 kg	88 lb /40 kg
White rice	2 tbsp /20 g	3 tbsp /35 g	¼ cup /45 g	¼ cup plus 2 tsp/55 g	⅜ cup /75 g	½ cup /95 g
Parmesan cheese, grated	4 tsp /20 g	⅜ cup /35 g	½ cup /45 g	⅔ cup /55 g	⅞ cup /75 g	1 cup /95 g
Pork fat/lard	1 tsp	2 tsp	2 tbsp	1 tbsp	4 tsp	5 tsp
Beef	3½ oz /100 g	6 oz /170 g	8⅛ oz /230 g	10 oz /285 g	13½ oz /385 g	1 lb ¾ oz /475 g
Sunflower oil	1 scant tsp	1 tsp	2 tsp	2 tsp	1 tbsp	3½ tsp
Flaxseed (linseed) oil	1 scant tsp	1 tsp	2 tsp	2 tsp	1 tbsp	3½ tsp
Salmon oil	1 scant tsp	1 tsp	2 tsp	2 tsp	1 tbsp	3½ tsp
Supplement	2 tsp /5 g	1 tbsp + ⅓ tsp/8 g	1 tbsp + 2⅓ tsp /11 g	Scant 2 tbsp/14 g	2 tbsp + 1⅔ tsp /19 g	3 tbsp + ⅓ tsp /24 g
Apples, unpeeled, diced	½ cup /50 g	¾ cup /85 g	1 cup /115 g	1¼ cups /140 g	1¾ cups /190 g	2¼ cups /240 g

NUTRITION PER 3½ OZ/100 G

MACRONUTRIENTS

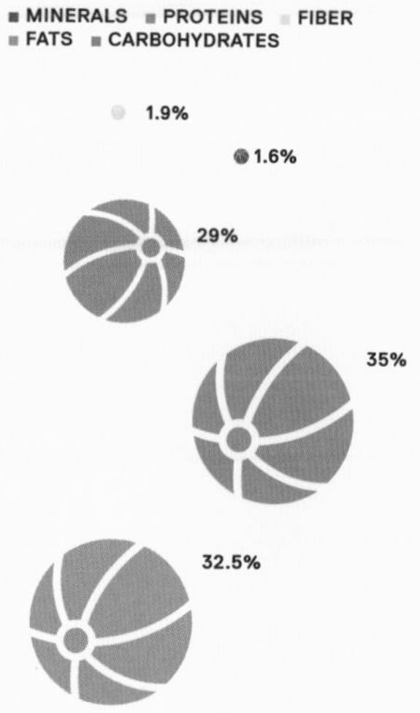
■ MINERALS ■ PROTEINS ■ FIBER
■ FATS ■ CARBOHYDRATES
1.9%
1.6%
29%
35%
32.5%

Beef with Vegetables and Ginger

P. 100

DAILY QUANTITY

INGREDIENTS	WEIGHT OF DOG					
Dog Weight	11 lb /5 kg	22 lb /10 kg	33 lb /15 kg	44 lb /20 kg	66 lb /30 kg	88 lb /40 kg
Fatty beef	2½ oz /70 g	4⅓ oz /125 g	6 oz /170 g	7⅓ oz /210 g	10 oz /285 g	12¾ oz /360 g
Carrots, diced	2 tbsp /30 g	⅓ cup /50 g	½ cup /70 g	⅔ cup /85 g	¾ cup /115 g	1 cup /145 g
Zucchini (courgette), diced	1¼ cups /30 g	2½ cups /50 g	2¾ cups /70 g	3⅓ cups /85 g	4⅔ cups /115 g	5¾ cups /145 g
White rice	3 tbsp /35 g	⅓ cup /60 g	⅜ cup /80 g	½ cup /100 g	¾ cup /135 g	⅞ cup /170 g
Sunflower oil	½ tsp	1 tsp	1 tsp	1½ tsp	2 tsp	2½ tsp
Coconut oil	Scant ½ tsp	½ tsp	1 scant tsp	1 tsp	1½ tsp	2 tsp
Flaxseed (linseed) oil	½ tsp	1 tsp	1 tsp	1½ tsp	2 tsp	2½ tsp
Supplement	Generous tsp/3 g	2 tsp /5 g	1 tbsp /7 g	1 tbsp + ½ tsp /9 g	1 tbsp + 1½ tsp /11 g	2 tbsp /14 g
Parmesan cheese	2 tsp /5 g	1 tbsp /8 g	4 tsp /10 g	2 scant tbsp/15 g	6 tsp /20 g	3 tbsp /25 g
Ginger, ground	¼ tsp /1 g	⅓ tsp /2 g	⅓ tsp /2 g	½ tsp /3 g	1 tsp /4 g	1¼ tsp /5 g

NUTRITION PER 3½ OZ/100 G

MACRONUTRIENTS

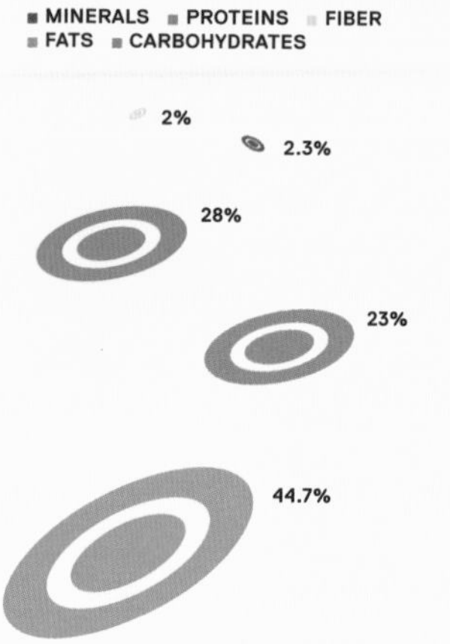
■ MINERALS ■ PROTEINS ■ FIBER
■ FATS ■ CARBOHYDRATES
2%
2.3%
28%
23%
44.7%

Multi-Layered Brown Rice

P. 102

DAILY QUANTITY

INGREDIENTS	WEIGHT OF DOG					
Dog Weight	11 lb /5 kg	22 lb /10 kg	33 lb /15 kg	44 lb /20 kg	66 lb /30 kg	88 lb /40 kg
Brown rice	¼ cup /45 g	⅓ cup /75 g	½ cup /100 g	⅔ cup /125 g	⅞ cup /175 g	1⅛ cups /215 g
Salmon	1¼ oz /35 g	2⅛ oz /60 g	2⅞ oz /80 g	3½ oz /100 g	4¾ oz /135 g	5⅞ oz /165 g
Squash, diced	1½ tbsp /12 g	¼ cup /35 g	⅓ cup /45 g	⅜ cup /55 g	½ cup /75 g	¾ cup /95 g
Turkey	⅞ oz /25 g	1⅜ oz /40 g	2⅛ oz /60 g	2½ oz /70 g	3⅜ oz /95 g	4¼ oz /120 g
Veal	⅞ oz /25 g	1⅜ oz /40 g	2⅛ oz /60 g	2½ oz /70 g	3⅜ oz /95 g	4¼ oz /120 g
Supplement	1⅔ tsp /4 g	Scant tbsp /7 g	1 tbsp + ⅔ tsp /9 g	1 tbsp + 2⅓ tsp /11 g	2 tbsp /15 g	2 tbsp + 1⅔ tsp /19 g
Corn oil	½ tsp	1 tsp	2 tsp	2½ tsp	1 tbsp	4 tsp

NUTRITION PER 3½ OZ/100 G

MACRONUTRIENTS

■ MINERALS ■ PROTEINS ■ FIBER
■ FATS ■ CARBOHYDRATES

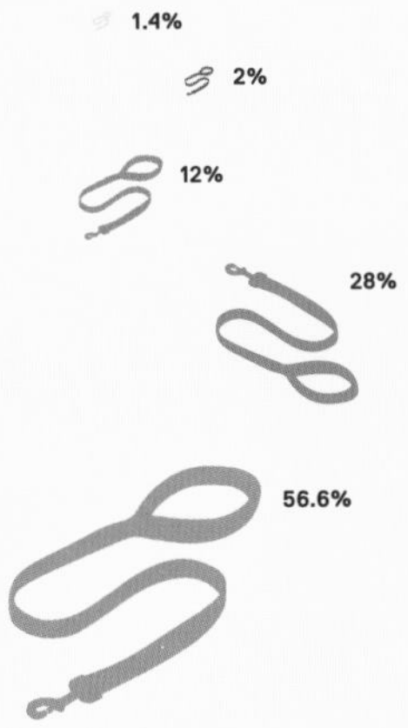

1.4%
2%
12%
28%
56.6%

Stew with Beans, Rice, and Berries

P. 103

DAILY QUANTITY

INGREDIENTS	WEIGHT OF DOG					
Dog Weight	11 lb /5 kg	22 lb /10 kg	33 lb /15 kg	44 lb /20 kg	66 lb /30 kg	88 lb /40 kg
Puffed rice	2 cups /30 g	3½ cups /50 g	5 cups /70 g	6 cups /85 g	8¼ cups /115 g	10⅓ cups /145 g
Chicken	1½ oz /45 g	2⅜ oz /75 g	3¾ oz /105 g	4½ oz /130 g	6¼ oz /175 g	7½ oz /215 g
Green beans, chopped	4 tbsp /35 g	½ cup /60 g	¾ cup /80 g	⅞ cup /100 g	1¼ cups /135 g	1½ cups /165 g
Veal	1½ oz /45 g	2⅜ oz /75 g	3¾ oz /105 g	4½ oz /130 g	6¼ oz /175 g	7½ oz /215 g
Supplement	1⅔ tsp /4 g	Scant tbsp /7 g	1 tbsp + ⅔ tsp /9 g	1 tbsp + 2⅓ tsp /11 g	2 tbsp /14 g	2 tbsp + 1⅔ tsp /19 g
Berries (blueberries, goji berries)	2 tsp /5 g	1 tbsp /8 g	2 tbsp /11 g	3 tbsp /14 g	3 tbsp /19 g	3½ tbsp /24 g
Sunflower oil	2 tsp	1 tbsp	4 tsp	5 tsp	2 tbsp	2½ tbsp

NUTRITION PER 3½ OZ/100 G

MACRONUTRIENTS

■ MINERALS ■ PROTEINS ■ FIBER
■ FATS ■ CARBOHYDRATES

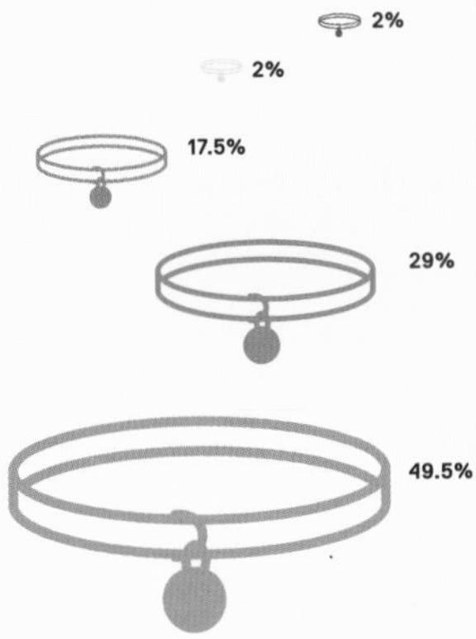

2%
2%
17.5%
29%
49.5%

Surf and Turf with Spirulina

P. 104

DAILY QUANTITY

INGREDIENTS	WEIGHT OF DOG					
Dog Weight	11 lb /5 kg	22 lb /10 kg	33 lb /15 kg	44 lb /20 kg	66 lb /30 kg	88 lb /40 kg
Fatty beef	1 oz /30 g	1¾ oz /50 g	2½ oz /70 g	3 oz /85 g	4 oz /115 g	5⅛ oz /145 g
Beef heart	¾ oz /20 g	1¼ oz /35 g	1½ oz /45 g	2 oz /55 g	2⅞ oz /80 g	3⅜ oz /95 g
Beef tripe	1 oz /30 g	1¾ oz /50 g	2½ oz /70 g	3 oz /85 g	4 oz /115 g	5⅛ oz /145 g
Carrots, grated	½ cup /50 g	¾ cup /85 g	1 cup /115 g	1¼ cups /140 g	1¾ cups /190 g	2⅓ cups /240 g
Pumpkin seed flour	1 scant tsp/5 g	1 tsp /10 g	1 tsp /10 g	2½ tsp /15 g	1 tbsp /20 g	1¼ tbsp /25 g
Spirulina powder	1 tsp/2 g	1 ½ tsp /3 g	2 tsp/5 g	2½ tsp /6 g	1 tbsp/8 g	4 tsp /10 g
Trout	1 oz /30 g	1¾ oz /50 g	2½ oz /70 g	3 oz /85 g	4 oz /115 g	5⅛ oz /145 g
Green beans	¼ cup /30 g	½ cup /50 g	⅔ cup /70 g	¾ cup /85 g	1 cup /115 g	1⅓ cup /145 g
Sunflower oil	2 tsp	3 ½ tsp	4 ½ tsp	2 tbsp	7½ tsp	3 tbsp plus 1 tsp
Supplement	Scant tsp /2 g	Generous tsp/3 g	2 tsp/5 g	21/2 tsp /6 g	Generous tbsp/8 g	1 tbsp + 1 tsp/10 g
Parmesan cheese, grated	2 tbsp /10 g	3 cup /15 g	¼ cup /25 g	⅓ cup /30 g	½ cup /40 g	⅔cup /50 g
Pine nuts	2 tsp	1 tbsp	1½ tbsp	2 tbsp	3 scant tbsp	3 generous tbsp

NUTRITION PER 3½ OZ/100 G

MACRONUTRIENTS

■ MINERALS ■ PROTEINS ■ FIBER
■ FATS ■ CARBOHYDRATES

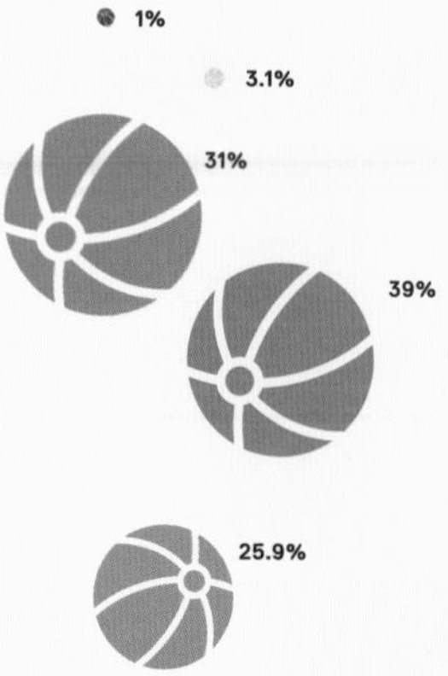
1%
3.1%
31%
39%
25.9%

Tartare Trio

P. 106

DAILY QUANTITY

INGREDIENTS	WEIGHT OF DOG					
Dog Weight	11 lb /5 kg	22 lb /10 kg	33 lb /15 kg	44 lb /20 kg	66 lb /30 kg	88 lb /40 kg
Chicken giblets	1 oz /30 g	1¾ oz /50 g	2½ oz /70 g	3 oz /85 g	4 oz /115 g	5⅛ oz /145 g
Carrots, grated	⅓ cup /40 g	⅔ cup /70 g	¾ cup /90 g	1 cup /115 g	1⅓ cups /155 g	1¾ cups /190 g
Supplement	1⅔ tsp/4 g	Scant tbsp/7 g	1 tbsp + ⅔ tsp/9 g	1 tbsp + 2⅔ tsp/11 g	2 tbsp /14 g	2 tbsp + 1⅔ tsp/19 g
Spirulina	¾ tsp/3 g	1 tsp/5 g	Generous tsp/7 g	Scant 2 tsp/8 g	2½ tsp /12 g	1 tbsp /14 g
Peas	3½ tbsp /30 g	⅓ cup /50 g	½ cup /70 g	⅔ cup /85 g	¾ cup /115 g	1 cup /145 g
Beef	1 oz /30 g	1¾ oz /50 g	2½ oz /70 g	3 oz /85 g	4 oz /115 g	5⅛ oz /145 g
Rabbit	1 oz /30 g	1½ oz /45 g	2¼ oz /65 g	2⅞ oz /80 g	3¾ oz /105 g	4¾ oz /135 g
Corn oil	½ tsp	1 tsp	1¼ tsp	1¼ tsp	¾ tbsp	1 tbsp
Salmon oil	½ tsp	Scant tsp	1 tsp	1¼ tsp	¾ tbsp	1 tbsp
Fresh salmon	¾ oz /20 g	1 oz /30 g	1¾ oz /40 g	1¾ oz /50 g	2½ oz /70 g	3 oz /85 g
Pine nuts	1 tsp/5 g	1 generous tsp/8 g	¾ tbsp /10 g	1 tbsp /15 g	1 ¼ tbsp /20 g	1½ tbsp /25 g
Pumpkin seeds	1 tsp /5 g	1½ tsp /7 g	1¾ tsp /11 g	1 tbsp /15 g	1½ tbsp /19 g	2½ tbsp /24 g

NUTRITION PER 3½ OZ/100 G

MACRONUTRIENTS

■ MINERALS ■ PROTEINS ■ FIBER
■ FATS ■ CARBOHYDRATES

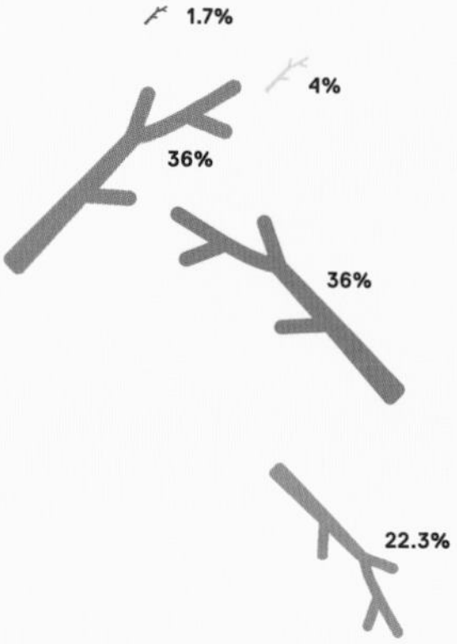
1.7%
4%
36%
36%
22.3%

Lamb and Cod with Egg

P. 107

DAILY QUANTITY

INGREDIENTS	WEIGHT OF DOG					
Dog Weight	11 lb /5 kg	22 lb /10 kg	33 lb /15 kg	44 lb /20 kg	66 lb /30 kg	88 lb /40 kg
Cod	1¾ oz /50 g	3 oz /85 g	4 oz /115 g	5 oz /140 g	6¾ oz /190 g	8½ oz /240 g
Lamb	1 oz /30 g	1¾ oz /50 g	2½ oz /70 g	3 oz /85 g	4 oz /115 g	5⅛ oz /145 g
Salmon oil	1 tsp	1½ tsp	2 tsp	2 tsp	1 tbsp	4 tsp
Spirulina powder	¾ tsp /5 g	1 tbsp /8 g	1½ tbsp /11 g	2 tbsp /14 g	2½ tbsp /19 g	3½ tbsp /24 g
Pumpkin seeds, roasted and ground	1 tbsp/5 g	1 generous tbsp /8 g	1½ tbsp /11 g	2 tbsp plus 1 tsp /14 g	3 tbsp /19 g	¼ cup /24 g
Carrots, diced	½ cup /70 g	⅞ cup /120 g	1⅛ cups /160 g	1⅜ cups /200 g	2 cups /270 g	2⅓ cups /335 g
Peas	⅓ cup /50 g	½ cup /85 g	¾ cup /115 g	1 cup /140 g	1⅓ cups /190 g	1⅔ cups /240 g
Eggs	¼ cup /55 g	⅓ cup /90 g	½ cup /120 g	⅔ cup /150 g	⅞ cup /205 g	1 cup /250 g
Pine nuts	2 tsp/5 g	1 tbsp/8 g	4 tsp/11 g	5 tsp/14 g	7 tsp/19 g	3 tbsp /24 g
Supplement	1⅔ tsp /4 g	Scant tbsp/7 g	1 tbsp + ⅔ tsp/9 g	1 tbsp + 2⅓ tsp/11 g	2 tbsp /14 g	2 tbsp + 1⅔ tsp/19 g
Corn oil	1 tsp	1½ tsp	2 tsp	2 tsp	1 tbsp	4 tsp

NUTRITION PER 3½ OZ/100 G

MACRONUTRIENTS

■ MINERALS ■ PROTEINS ■ FIBER
■ FATS ■ CARBOHYDRATES

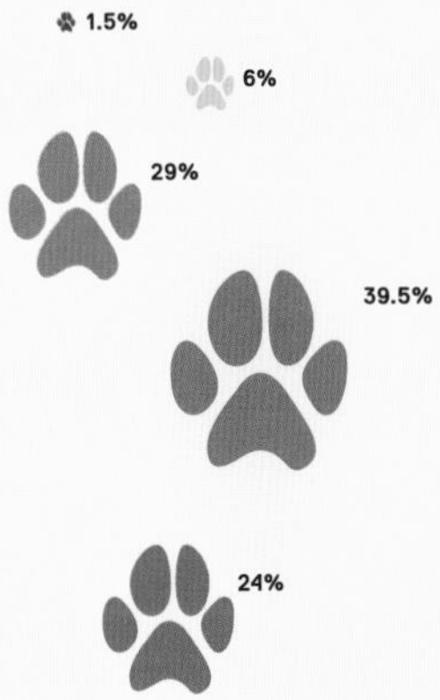

SENIOR DOG NUTRITION

Rice, Egg, and Vegetable Croquettes

P. 111

DAILY QUANTITY

INGREDIENTS	WEIGHT OF DOG					
Dog Weight	11 lb /5 kg	22 lb /10 kg	33 lb /15 kg	44 lb /20 kg	66 lb /30 kg	88 lb /40 kg
White rice	2½ tbsp /30 g	⅓ cup /65 g	½ cup /90 g	⅔ cup /115 g	⅞ cup /155 g	1 cup /190 g
Eggs	¼ cup /55 g	⅓ cup /90 g	½ cup /120 g	⅔ cup /150 g	⅞ cup /205 g	1 cup /250 g
Pumpkin or other squash, diced	3 tbsp /20 g	⅓ cup /35 g	⅜ cup /45 g	½ cup /60 g	¾ cup /80 g	⅞ cup /95 g
Parmesan cheese, grated	2 tbsp /10 g	3 tbsp /15 g	¼ cup /25 g	⅓ cup /30 g	½ cup /40 g	⅔ cup /50 g
Brewer's yeast or Marmite	1 tsp /4 g	1½ tsp /7 g	2 tsp /9 g	¾ tbsp /11 g	1 tbsp /15 g	1⅓ tsp /19 g
Carrots, thin strips	2½ tbsp /20 g	¼ cup /35 g	⅓ cup /45 g	⅜ cup /55 g	½ cup /80 g	⅔ cup /95 g
Coconut oil	Scant ½ tsp	½ tsp	1 scant tsp	1 tsp	1½ tsp	2 tsp
Sunflower oil	1 tsp	1½ tsp	2 tsp	¾ tbsp	1 tbsp	1⅓ tsp
Supplement	1⅕ tsp /3 g	2 tsp/5 g	Scant 1 tbsp/7 g	Generous 1 tbsp /8 g	1 tbsp + 1 tsp/12 g	2 tbsp /14 g
Carrots, thin strips	2½ tbsp /20 g	¼ cup /35 g	⅓ cup /45 g	⅜ cup /55 g	½ cup /80 g	⅔ cup /95 g

NUTRITION PER 3½ OZ/100 G

MACRONUTRIENTS

■ MINERALS ■ PROTEINS ■ FIBER
■ FATS ■ CARBOHYDRATES

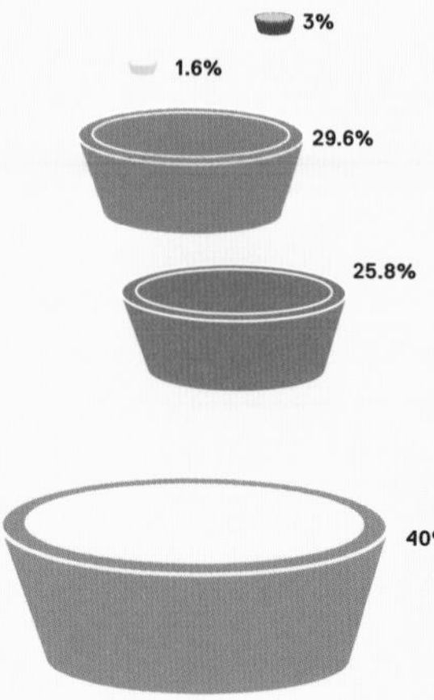
3%
1.6%
29.6%
25.8%
40%

Pasta with Smashed Eggs

P. 112

DAILY QUANTITY

INGREDIENTS	WEIGHT OF DOG					
Dog Weight	11 lb /5 kg	22 lb /10 kg	33 lb /15 kg	44 lb /20 kg	66 lb /30 kg	88 lb /40 kg
Wholegrain pasta	1 oz /30 g	1⅜ oz /50 g	2½ oz /70 g	3 oz /85 g	4 oz /115 g	5⅛ oz /145 g
Butter	½ tsp /2 g	¾ tsp /3 g	1¼ tsp /5 g	1⅓ tsp /6 g	1¾ tsp /8 g	2 tbsp /10 g
Pumpkin or other winter squash, diced	¼ cup /30 g	⅓ cup /50 g	½ cup /70 g	⅔ cup /85 g	⅞ cup /115 g	1⅛ cups /145 g
Carrots, diced	3 tbsp /30 g	⅓ cup /50 g	Scant ½ cup/70 g	½ cup /85 g	¾ cup /115 g	1 cup /145 g
Beef lung	1 oz /30 g	⅜ oz /50 g	2½ oz /70 g	3 oz /85 g	4 oz /115 g	5⅛ oz /145 g
Eggs	¼ cup /40 g	½ cup /65 g	⅔ cup /90 g	⅞ cup /115 g	1⅛ cups /155 g	1⅓ cups /190 g
Coconut oil	1 tsp	1½ tsp	2 tsp	2½ tsp	1 tbsp	1½ tbsp
Flaxseed (linseed) oil	1 tsp	1½ tsp	2 tsp	2½ tsp	1 tbsp	1½ tbsp
Salmon oil	½ tsp	¾ tsp	1¼ tsp	1⅓ tsp	1¾ tsp	2 tsp
Supplement	1¼ tsp /3 g	2 tsp/5 g	Scant 1 tbsp/7 g	Generous 1 tbsp/8 g	1 tbsp + 1½ tsp /12 g	2 tbsp /14 g

NUTRITION PER 3½ OZ/100 G

MACRONUTRIENTS

■ MINERALS ■ PROTEINS ■ FIBER
■ FATS ■ CARBOHYDRATES

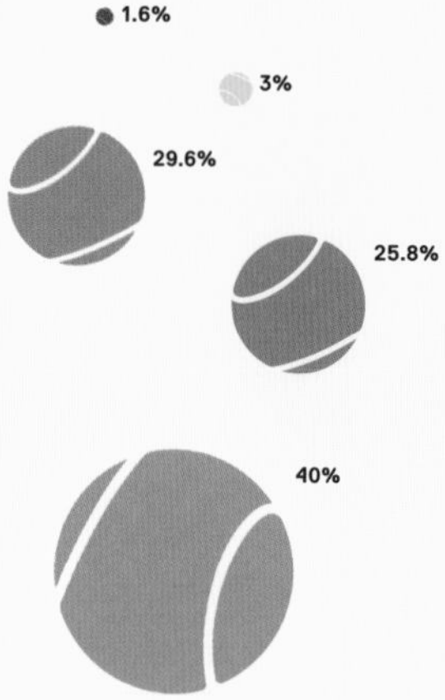
1.6%
3%
29.6%
25.8%
40%

Rice Zuccotto with Turkey

P. 114

DAILY QUANTITY

INGREDIENTS	WEIGHT OF DOG					
Dog Weight	11 lb /5 kg	22 lb /10 kg	33 lb /15 kg	44 lb /20 kg	66 lb /30 kg	88 lb /40 kg
Turkey breast	2¼ oz /65 g	3⅞ oz /110 g	5⅛ oz /150 g	6½ oz /185 g	8¾ oz /250 g	11 oz /310 g
White rice	2½ tbsp /30 g	⅓ cup /60 g	⅜ cup /75 g	½ cup /95 g	¾ cup /130 g	⅞ cup /160 g
Chicory	½ cup /60 g	scant ¾ cup /100 g	1 cup /135 g	1¼ cups /170 g	1⅔ cups /230 g	2¼ cups /285 g
Green beans	½ cup /60 g	⅞ cup /100 g	1 scant cup/135 g	1¼ cups /170 g	2 cups /230 g	2½ cups /285 g
Corn oil	¾ tsp	1½ tsp	1 tbsp	1¼ tbsp	2½ tbsp	2 tbsp
Supplement	1⅔ tsp /4 g	1 scant tbsp/7 g	1 tbsp + ⅔ tsp/9 g	1 tbsp + 1 tsp/11 g	2 tbsp + ½ tsp/15 g	2½ tbsp /19 g

NUTRITION PER 3½ OZ/100 G

MACRONUTRIENTS

■ MINERALS ■ PROTEINS ■ FIBER
■ FATS ■ CARBOHYDRATES

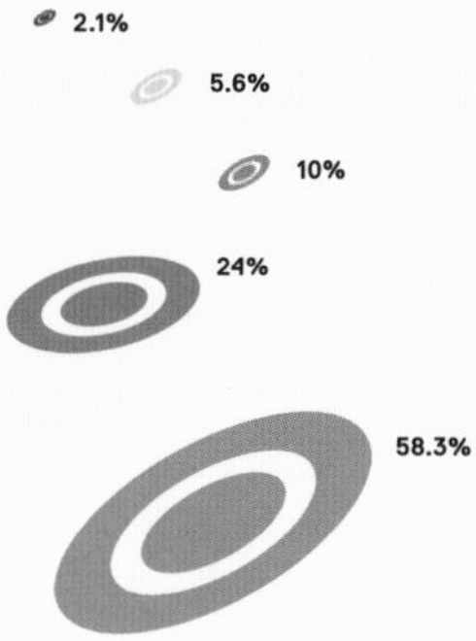
2.1%
5.6%
10%
24%
58.3%

Turmeric Rice with Turkey

P. 115

DAILY QUANTITY

INGREDIENTS	WEIGHT OF DOG					
Dog Weight	11 lb /5 kg	22 lb /10 kg	33 lb /15 kg	44 lb /20 kg	66 lb /30 kg	88 lb /40 kg
Turkey breast	2⅛ oz /60 g	3½ oz /100 g	5 oz /140 g	6 oz /170 g	8⅛ oz /230 g	10 oz /285 g
Brown rice	¼ cup /40 g	⅓ cup /65 g	½ cup /90 g	⅔ cup /115 g	¾ cup /155 g	1 cup /190 g
White potatoes, diced	½ cup /80 g	⅞ cup /135 g	1½ cups /180 g	1¾ cups /225 g	2⅓ cups /305 g	3 cups /380 g
Turmeric	1 g	2 g	2 g	3 g	4 g	5 g
Corn oil	½ tsp	1 tsp	1 tsp	1½ tsp	2 tsp	2½ tsp
Supplement	1⅔ tsp /4 g	1 scant tbsp/7 g	1 tbsp + ⅔ tsp/9 g	1 tbsp + 1 tsp/11 g	2 tbsp + ½ tsp/15 g	2½ tbsp /19 g

NUTRITION PER 3½ OZ/100 G

MACRONUTRIENTS

■ MINERALS ■ PROTEINS ■ FIBER
■ FATS ■ CARBOHYDRATES

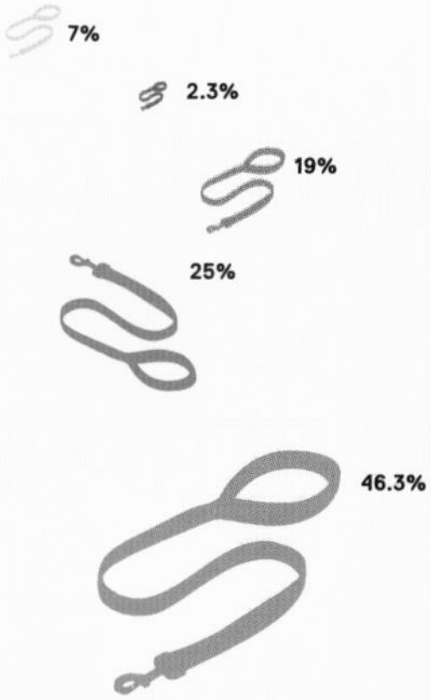
7%
2.3%
19%
25%
46.3%

Vegetable Cream with Croutons

P. 117

DAILY QUANTITY

INGREDIENTS	WEIGHT OF DOG					
Dog Weight	11 lb /5 kg	22 lb /10 kg	33 lb /15 kg	44 lb /20 kg	66 lb /30 kg	88 lb /40 kg
Turkey thigh, skinless	1¾ oz /50 g	3 oz /85 g	4 oz /115 g	5 oz /140 g	6¾ oz /190 g	8½ oz /240 g
White bread	1 slice /20 g	1⅓ slices /35 g	1¾ slices /45 g	2 slices /55 g	3 slices /75 g	4 slices /95 g
Plain nonfat yogurt	⅓ cup /80 ml	⅔ cup /135 ml	¾ cup /180 ml	1 cup /230 ml	1⅓ cups /310 ml	1⅔ cups /380 ml
Coconut oil	1 scant tsp	1 tsp	1½ tsp	2 tsp	1 tbsp	3½ tsp
Salmon oil	1 scant tsp	1 tsp	1½ tsp	2 tsp	1 tbsp	3½ tsp
Rolled oats	2 tbsp /10 g	2½ tbsp /15 g	¼ cup /20 g	⅓ cup /30 g	⅜ cup /40 g	½ cup /50 g
Pumpkin or other squash, diced	3 tbsp /20 g	⅓ cup /35 g	⅜ cup /45 g	½ cup /55 g	⅔ cup /75 g	⅞ cup /95 g
Carrots, diced	2½ tbsp /20 g	¼ cup /35 g	⅓ cup /45 g	⅜ cup /55 g	½ cup /75 g	⅔ cup /95 g
Flaxseed (linseed) oil	1 tsp	1½ tsp	2¼ tsp	2¾ tsp	1 tbsp	4 tsp
Supplement	2 tsp/5 g	Generous tbsp/8 g	1 tbsp + 1 tsp/11 g	2 tbsp /14 g	2½ tbsp /19 g	3 tbsp + 1 tsp/24 g

NUTRITION PER 3½ OZ/100 G

MACRONUTRIENTS

■ MINERALS ■ PROTEINS ■ FIBER
■ FATS ■ CARBOHYDRATES

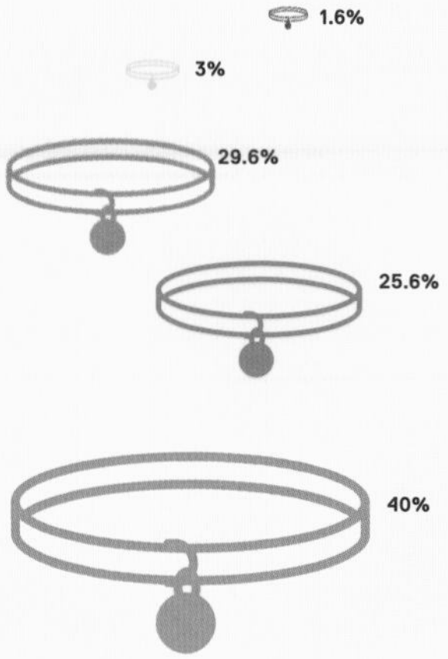
1.6%
3%
29.6%
25.6%
40%

Tapioca with Pork and Carrots

P. 119

DAILY QUANTITY

INGREDIENTS	WEIGHT OF DOG					
Dog Weight	11 lb /5 kg	22 lb /10 kg	33 lb /15 kg	44 lb /20 kg	66 lb /30 kg	88 lb /40 kg
Pork neck or shoulder	2½ oz /70 g	4¼ oz /120 g	5⅝ oz /160 g	7 oz /200 g	9½ oz /270 g	11¾ oz /335 g
Pig's liver	¾ oz /20 g	1¼ oz /35 g	1½ oz /45 g	2 oz /55 g	2⅝ oz /75 g	3⅜ oz /95 g
Tapioca	¼ cup /40 g	½ cup /65 g	⅔ cup /90 g	¾ cup /115 g	1 cup /155 g	1¼ cups /190 g
Carrots, grated	¼ cup /30 g	½ cup /50 g	⅔ cup /70 g	¾ cup /85 g	1 cup /115 g	1⅓ cups /145 g
Sunflower oil	½ tsp	1 tsp	1¼ tsp	1½ tsp	2 tsp	2½ tsp
Supplement	1⅔ tsp /4 g	1 scant tbsp/7 g	1 tbsp + ⅔ tsp/9 g	1 tbsp + 1 tsp/11 g	2 tbsp + ½ tsp/15 g	2½ tbsp /19 g

NUTRITION PER 3½ OZ/100 G

MACRONUTRIENTS

■ MINERALS ■ PROTEINS ■ FIBER
■ FATS ■ CARBOHYDRATES

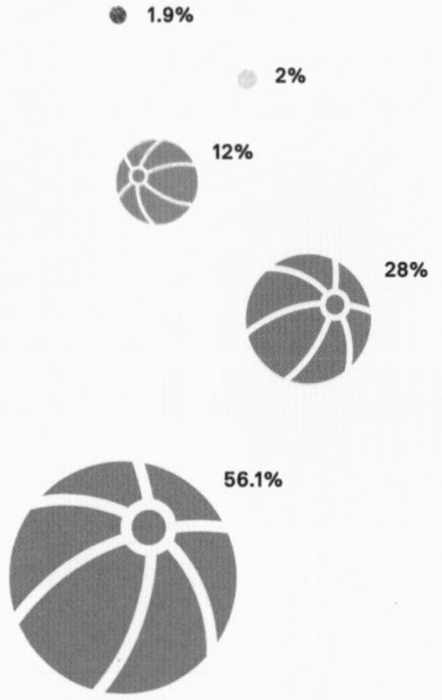
1.9%
2%
12%
28%
56.1%

Quinoa with Squash and Lamb Ragù

P. 120

DAILY QUANTITY

INGREDIENTS	WEIGHT OF DOG					
Dog Weight	11 lb /5 kg	22 lb /10 kg	33 lb /15 kg	44 lb /20 kg	66 lb /30 kg	88 lb /40 kg
Lamb	1¾ oz /50 g	3 oz /85 g	4 oz /115 g	5 oz /140 g	6¾ oz /190 g	8½ oz /240 g
Quinoa	¼ cup /50 g	½ cup /85 g	⅔ cup /115 g	¾ cup /140 g	1⅛ cups /190 g	1⅓ cups /240 g
Squash, finely diced	3 tbsp /20 g	⅓ cup /35 g	⅜ cup /45 g	½ cup /55 g	⅔ cup /75 g	⅞ cup /95 g
Corn oil	½ tsp	1 tsp	1 tsp	1½ tsp	2 tsp	1 tbsp
Supplement	1⅔ tsp /4 g	1 scant tbsp/7 g	1 tbsp + ⅔ tsp/9 g	1 tbsp + 1 tsp/11 g	2 tbsp + ½ tsp/15 g	2½ tbsp /19 g

NUTRITION PER 3½ OZ/100 G

MACRONUTRIENTS

■ MINERALS ■ PROTEINS ■ FIBER ■ FATS ■ CARBOHYDRATES

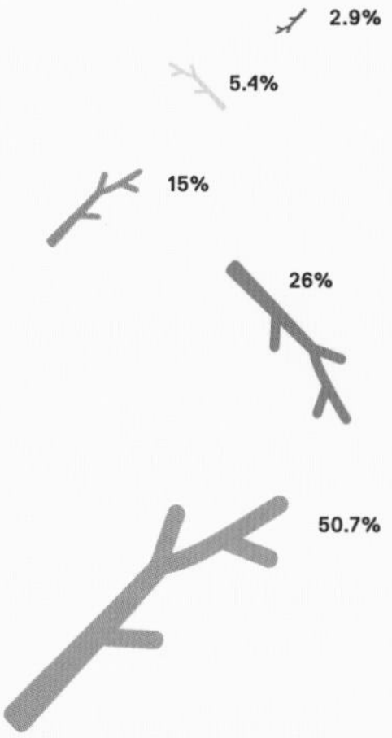
2.9%
5.4%
15%
26%
50.7%

Coconut-Scented Couscous

P. 123

DAILY QUANTITY

INGREDIENTS	WEIGHT OF DOG					
Dog Weight	11 lb /5 kg	22 lb /10 kg	33 lb /15 kg	44 lb /20 kg	66 lb /30 kg	88 lb /40 kg
Pork neck or shoulder	2 oz /55 g	3⅛ oz /90 g	4⅜ oz /125 g	5½ oz /155 g	7⅜ oz /210 g	9⅛ oz /260 g
Couscous	¼ cup /45 g	⅜ cup /75 g	⅔ cup /105 g	¾ cup /130 g	1 cup /170 g	1¼ cups /215 g
Chicken giblets	½ oz /15 g	⅞ oz /25 g	1¼ oz /35 g	1⅜ oz /40 g	2⅛ oz /60 g	3½ oz /70 g
Coconut oil	½ tsp	½ tsp	1 tsp	1 tsp	1½ tsp	2 tsp
Sunflower oil	½ tsp	½ tsp	1 tsp	1 tsp	1½ tsp	2 tsp
Supplement	1⅔ tsp /4 g	1 scant tbsp/7 g	1 tbsp + ⅔ tsp/9 g	1 tbsp + 1 tsp/11 g	2 tbsp + ½ tsp/15 g	2½ tbsp /19 g

NUTRITION PER 3½ OZ/100 G

MACRONUTRIENTS

■ MINERALS ■ PROTEINS ■ FIBER ■ FATS ■ CARBOHYDRATES

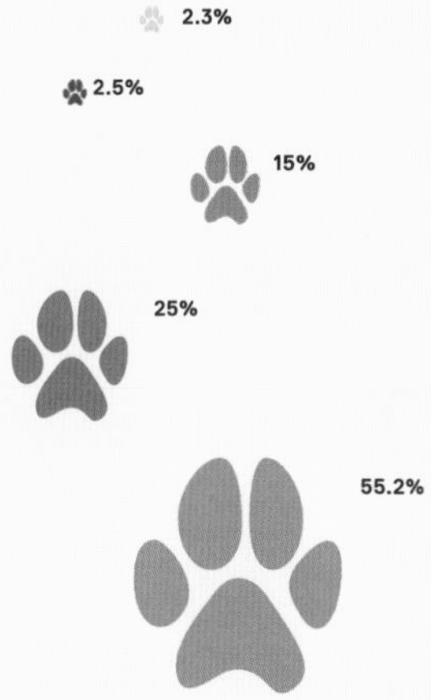
2.3%
2.5%
15%
25%
55.2%

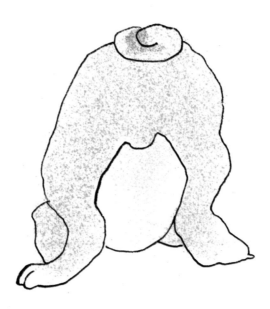

DIET IN DETAIL

Dogs and Their Diets

The first thing to consider when preparing a diet plan for your dog is the balance of nutrients that each meal will provide. Knowing this means that your dog's needs can be met, and excesses and deficiencies avoided; this is important as dogs aren't capable of regulating this themselves. Although each and every recipe in this book is perfectly balanced for dogs, this is why we've included basic nutritional values per 3¼ oz/100g (see pages 44–122) for each recipe.

The two main reasons dogs can't regulate their own food intake are:

- Instinct: dogs are descended from wolves, which are prone to eating more than they actually need. As hunters, the ancestors of the domestic dog couldn't predict when, or how much, they would and could eat, so they adapted, stocking up on energy whenever possible.
- Breeding: many breeds became popular because they would eat anything they were given, meaning they are less able to regulate their food intake.

The energy and nutritional needs of a dog will change depending on what stage of life it's at, and how much physical activity it engages in. Taking these things into consideration is essential for ensuring the most appropriate diet.

PUPPYHOOD

At this stage, dogs are growing and nutrition plays a fundamental role. This is a particularly delicate stage to manage in terms of correct weight, because puppies need to take in many nutrients to reach their adult size and become fully grown sexually, but at the same time their gastrointestinal system isn't fully developed.

ADULT DOGS

Adult dogs' food requirements can be defined as one of "maintenance". During reproduction, female dogs have specific requirements linked to their gestation and production of milk. See page 175 for more information. Sterilization, an operation that many dogs have, causes significant metabolic changes; there is a decrease of lean mass and an increase of fat mass, which means a lower energy requirement. With the same weight a dog, once neutered, will have lower metabolic requirements and, therefore, different maintenance requirements. If your dog is struggling to maintain a healthy weight, choose the 'light' dishes within the recipe section.

SENIOR DOGS

More than a stage, aging is a lifelong process, during which there is a progressive decline in the body's functions. However, we only become aware of this decline when the first symptoms of old age appear; these include muscle loss, less physical activity, and a gradual loss of sight and hearing. The age at which these symptoms occur varies from dog to dog and is inextricably linked to size: in general, it begins earlier in large breeds and later in smaller breeds. See page 178 to find out whether your dog qualifies as a senior.

The Diet of a Puppy

It is obvious that the genetic heritage transmitted by parents to puppies decisively conditions their appearance as adults. However, environmental factors also contribute to influencing this: first, of course, is nutrition, which plays a fundamental role not only on body development, but also in regard to the immunization against certain diseases and, in general, on the dog's future state of health. A characteristic, however, that is common to all puppies is their very rapid growth: in about eight days they will have doubled their birth weight, something that for other animals takes weeks, or even months. Adult weight, on the other hand, is reached, depending on the breed, at between six and 20 months.

WEANING PUPPIES

The weaning process takes the dog from a milk-based diet to solid food. Today, the trend at this stage is to overfeed puppies in the erroneous belief that "super dogs" will be the result or, simply, because their owners wish to see their dogs a little plumper. This approach has many negative effects: it makes the dog prone to obesity, gives it a tendency to be too demanding for food and can lead to the onset of bone diseases. It's common knowledge that to obtain good bone structure, the proper provision of mineral salts (calcium, phosphorus, magnesium, etc.), proteins, energy and some vitamins, are needed; but few people take into account the necessary time for the dog's natural development and force the animal to grow too fast, ultimately affecting correct bone formation. It is therefore necessary to find a balance between the rate of growth and diet.

DAILY FOOD AMOUNTS		
Stage of Life	Age	Daily Meals
Weaning	2–4 months	4
Growth stage	5–7 months	3
Adulthood	>7 months	2

In the wild, female canines give birth in the shelter of dens or natural hollows. In the period immediately following the birth, they stay in close contact with the litter, warming their puppies until they are able to regulate their body temperature independently. The hunting is left to the males, at least for a few weeks; even when the females return to hunting for food, another member of the pack – usually a young female – guards the den. Meanwhile, the puppies grow to the point at which the mother's milk is not enough to meet their needs; this is the start of the weaning process. The parents catch the prey, eat large quantities of it and, when they return to the den, each regurgitates the contents of their stomachs, which is then eaten by the puppies. This allows considerable quantities of food to be transported over long distances, and the food is altered by the gastric juices of the adults, making it more digestible, gently acclimatizing the puppies to new foods.

Instinct obviously determines certain behaviors, and it is therefore inevitable that some domesticated female dogs may act in a similar way. So regurgitation is a completely natural practice which should not cause aversion or concern, nor should it be stopped.

THE GROWTH STAGE OF PUPPIES

Over the weeks, not only do puppies grow by putting on mass, but the shape and structure of their organs also changes. It is the breed that, to a certain extent, will define growth rate: it is fastest during the period from birth to weaning, gradually decreasing until puberty; thereafter, the growth rate slows still more until it reaches adulthood. The time this process takes is proportional to what size the adult dog will be: it will take a large dog longer to reach full size than a small dog.

Food plays a fundamental role. The correct diet not only helps puppies reach the size appropriate to their respective genetic potential but also to become healthy adults.

Dogs at this stage are particularly sensitive to any imbalances or food deficiencies and, due to the high requirements dictated by their growth rate, they have low energy and nutrient reserves. For all of these reasons it is a good idea to pay particular attention to any diet plan for puppies. Large breeds deserve special attention as they are prone to the development of orthopedic diseases more than other dogs if their diet has an excessive or deficient energy intake, vitamin D, calcium, and phosphorus intake, or imbalances of calcium and phosphorus. The recipes in this book for puppies are a good starting point, but please consult your veterinarian for further information and advice regarding calculating exact energy requirements.

THE DIET OF A PUPPY

Meat and fish are two ingredients that can't be omitted from the diets of puppies; this is because, compared to adult dogs, their protein needs are higher and puppies require more specific essential amino acids. Unlike adult dogs, puppies are not fully capable of autonomously synthetizing all fatty acids. For adult dogs, only linoleic acid need to be included in their diet, while it is essential to include in a wider range of fatty acids found in animal fat, vegetable oil, fish oil, or krill oil in puppy's diets.

Deficiencies of eicosapentaenoic acid (EPA) and docosahexaenoic acid (DHA), types of mega-3 fatty acids found in oily fish and fish oils, are particularly dangerous, as they can lead to the development of non-optimal nervous tissue with consequent sight problems (due to retinal disorders), or insufficient brain development with consequent learning difficulties (a condition that is difficult to identify in dogs).

The Diet of an Adult Dog

A good starting point in creating a balanced diet for your dog may be to consider the foods that it would naturally and freely choose; this will give you an idea of what nutrients it needs and which can be part of its diet. An analysis such as this shows that a dog is an omnivorous animal with a digestive system that has adapted to a wide range of foods to obtain what is necessary in a balanced meal, namely:

- energy in a quantity equal to that released by its body in the form of heat, metabolism, and exercise; that which is retained in its tissues during its growth stage; or that which is transferred during pregnancy or nursing
- proteins and essential amino acids, minerals, vitamins and essential fatty acids, in sufficient quantities to cover its everyday needs
- fiber to ensure its digestive system functions properly

Over the years the nutrients your dog needs will remain the same, but the relative quantities—which will vary according to its physiological needs—must be reviewed, as they must if your dog develops a condition or illness.

THE DIET FOR A NEUTERED ADULT DOG

An overweight dog is a problem that owners of neutered dogs know well. After the operation, dogs often have a considerably increased appetite that does not, in fact, correspond to a real energy requirement. The physiological decrease of lean mass after the operation actually results in a decrease in the energy intake needed. A vicious circle is established that often results in weight problems.

To remedy this situation, it needs to be tackled from different angles:

- after the operation, it is a good idea to reduce their total energy intake by 20 percent
- despite the hormonal changes, it is important to increase your dog's physical activity to maintain lean mass
- include a lot of fiber in its diet (as this will stimulate a feeling of fullness) as well as more protein which activates its metabolism and helps to burn more calories

Your dog's diet must therefore be higher in vegetables such as chicory, pumpkin, and carrots, but also eggs, fish, legumes, and ricotta. Meat, red meat, in particular, is good because in addition to its high level of protein it is also high in carnitine, an effective amino acid that helps to maintain lean mass. Finally, it is also a good idea to include a wholegrain cereal such as some types of rice, which provides fiber and stabilizes blood sugar level, and thus helps to contain the feeling of hunger.

THE DIET FOR AN ADULT DOG IN ITS REPRODUCTIVE STAGE

Diet also plays a fundamental role when it comes to reproduction, both in its qualitative aspects (affecting hormonal balance and therefore fertility) as well as quantitatively (affecting the growth of the fetuses and production of milk). It is therefore vital that the proper diet be given to your dog at every stage of reproduction—mating, gestation, nursing, and post-nursing. As diet changes are quite specific during this time, we recommend that you see your veterinarian or nutrition specialist.

The Diet of Senior Dogs

At around the age of 10, the first signs of aging begin to show with the appearance of a dog's first white hairs; a slight loss of balance when it walks; and dogs starting to look more tired than they used to. Your dog is entering a new stage of its life, one in which which it may be more prone to illness and ailment.

Diet again plays a fundamental role. It has been proven that it is possible to slow down the aging process through proper feeding.

IS MY DOG OLD?

We all know that old age can't be reduced to statistics, but it's generally agreed that, for dogs, the turning point is usually around the age of 10. There are many variables that can determine their state of health; lifestyle and genetic factors being the main ones. Life expectancy is higher among small dogs—who are considered to be old from the age of 12, compared to 8 for larger dogs—and there are some breeds with longer lifespans than others: Pomeranians, for example, can live to 20.

Small dogs	12 years
Medium dogs	10 years
Large dogs	8 years

THE RIGHT INGREDIENT FOR EVERY NEED

With the onset of old age, home-cooking proves to be a particularly good ally to better satisfy any new needs your dog might develop. If it's already used to homemade food, adapting to a new diet can be a very natural process; if not, it's recommendable to make the transition gradually and with the supervision of a veterinary nutritionist. The measures to be applied, and the ingredients that will help your dog most will vary case-to-case:

• Loss of muscle mass: this is a problem mainly in male dogs and generally affects their head and thigh muscles. To prevent this loss, their food should be enhanced with proteins that have a high biological value. These are foods of animal origin such as meat, fish, eggs and ricotta, the quantities of which in their diet should be increased. Animal proteins are preferable for senior dogs due to their high biological value and for easier digestion than plant-based proteins.

- Loss of smell: this disorder is due to the degeneration of olfactory mucosa. Among the main consequences of this is a loss of interest in food. To get the dog in question to enjoy eating again, give it meals with a higher fat content, which will enhance the release of aromas which are increased when the food is heated to 86–95°F (30–35°C).
- Arthritis: age-related joint degeneration is another common symptom of old age. This is a disease that can't be cured; its symptoms, however, can be lessened through weight management. It's beneficial to include oil from oily fish such as krill and salmon in your dog's diet as these contain nutrients such as eicosapentaenoic acid (EPA). Including supplements containing substances like PEA (palmitoylethanolamide), glucosamine and chondroitin could be useful.
- Cognitive decline: in veterinary medicine it is called cognitive dysfunction syndrome (CDS) and can be spotted through small changes in daily behavior such as memory loss and a lowered ability to learn. Ultimately, it is a syndrome that, due to its development and symptomatology, can be compared to Alzheimer's.

THE FIRST SYMPTOMS OF OLD AGE

It is difficult to come to terms with the changes related to the cognitive decline of your dog and it's the one that's most upsetting for the dog's owner. The signs to look out for are many and varied. For example, you may get home one day and find a spot of urine on its bed, something that had never happened before; or you might notice a change in its sleep-wake rhythm; or it may develop a completely new and irritable stance towards other domestic animals.

Although the causes of this phenomenon have yet to be defined, the role of diet in reducing its effects has been amply demonstrated. It is therefore essential to add a variety of antioxidants to your dog's diet. These can be found in various foods: from extra-virgin olive oil to turmeric, from berries (blueberries, goji berries) to rosemary. The medium-chain triglycerides that are found in, for example, coconut oil, help to counteract cognitive dysfunction in senior dogs; and, adding omega-3 fatty acids to its food (found in the oil of oily fish and seafood such as salmon and krill) will have a specific, beneficial effect on learning, leading to an improvement in cognitive performance.

DISORDER	FOOD SOURCE
Loss of muscle mass	High-protein foods: meat, fish, eggs, ricotta
Loss of smell	Foods of animal origin high in fats
Arthrosis	Fish oil, krill or salmon
Cognitive dysfunction syndrome (CDS)	Antioxidants (extra-virgin olive oil, turmeric, berries, etc.); coconut oil; omega-3 (oil from oily fish and seafood such as salmon and krill)

→ KEY FACTORS FOR THE DIET OF A SENIOR DOG

→ **Make it appetizing: enhance the flavor and smell to make food more interesting.**

→ **Feed dogs high-protein foods to prevent the loss of lean mass, common in senior dogs.**

→ **Feed dogs an increased amount of antioxidants to prevent the action of free radicals.**

→ **Add MCT (medium-chain triglycerides)— particular fatty acids—found in coconut oil, which provide nutrition for brain tissue.**

Basic Nutritional Requirements

On page 18, the basic elements of a balanced diet were listed, but what are the components? In more technical terms, these break down into proteins, fats (or lipids), vitamins and minerals, and water. Carbohydrates—fiber in particular—should be looked at separately as, although they don't fall into the category of essential nutrients, they are still a good source of energy for dogs.

PROTEINS

Proteins are the basis of a dog's diet and those of animal origin —meat, fish, eggs, and cheese—are essential at certain stages of dogs' lives: they nourish puppies as they grow; help counteract the loss of muscle mass in senior dogs; and are needed at moments such as pregnancy and nursing, or during intense physical activity for adult dogs.

Plant-based proteins, mainly legumes, generally have a lower biological value because they're incomplete, i.e. are poor in some essential amino acids. Also, they're difficult for dogs to digest due to their very high fiber content. However, some legumes, such as peas, green beans, and soybeans are a good source of protein for dogs. Introducing these ingredients into their diets can be beneficial as they help to improve the regularity of digestion and, in the case of overweight dogs, supply protein that's low in calories. Only well cooked legumes should be given to dogs—especially soybeans, which would otherwise be toxic to them.

FATS (LIPIDS)

Commonly called 'fats', lipids are a very concentrated and efficient source of energy. What makes them truly indispensable to a dog's diet is both their central role in the absorption of some fat-soluble nutrients (such as vitamins A, D, E and K), which are fundamental to the wellbeing of the animal, and also the essential fatty acids (omega 6 and omega 3) they contain, which dogs' bodies don't produce. Broadly speaking, meat, cheese, dairy products, and eggs have high concentrations of omega 6, and fish, especially marine fish, are an important source of omega 3 (in particular DHA/EPA, which aren't present in plant-based oils). Dogs are able to digest and use plant-based fats such as extra-virgin olive oil, corn oil, sunflower and peanut oils that are an important source of omega 3, omega 6, fatty acid, and natural antioxidants, although not as effectively as animal fats.

Vitamins and minerals play an essential role in a dog's diet, but the quantities have to be measured with great care.

For adult dogs, the required amounts of these substances are relatively small; a dog's body is capable of storing them and thus minimizing their loss. However, it's easy for even the most varied homemade meals to be deficient in some way, so it's important to make this up with supplements (see page 208). The most obvious way that vitamins and minerals are lost is through cooking food: it's often necessary for eliminating harmful microorganisms and bacteria, but, inevitably it lowers the nutritional value of foods, leaving some vitamins inactive or reducing their effectiveness. Another case is that of calcium, which dogs ingest naturally when chewing bones. Despite this, including bones in a homemade diet isn't advisable, because it is very difficult to manage. In general, as dogs aren't weaned on prey (and, therefore, bones) they haven't developed the ability to chew this kind of food properly.

For this reason, and due to their shape—some bones are long and pointed while others are rounded and slippery—there's a high risk that they will perforate the gastrointestinal tract or block the intestines. Finally, from a nutritional standpoint, it's difficult to quantify the amount of calcium and other minerals which can be assimilated by the dog. This is a factor that varies depending on the kind of bone that's given to the dog (higher or lower in minerals depending on the age and type of animal from which they come).

As mentioned above, a lack of vitamins and minerals can cause problems for a dog's health but, conversely, too much can be harmful or even toxic. Supplements, too, must be balanced with great care; be careful, for example, not to give puppies too much calcium as this can lead to a series of skeletal diseases. Likewise, avoid too much of some foods to prevent vitamin overdose; for example, daily liver consumption higher than that suggested these recipes can lead to vitamin A and D toxicity.

BASIC NUTRITIONAL REQUIREMENTS

WATER

Water constitutes the base of the food pyramid, as well as being the main substance of dogs' bodies. Dogs can lose almost all of their fat and more than half of their proteins and still survive, but a loss of just 15 percent of their body water can be lethal to them. Under normal conditions, water is excreted in urine and feces, as well as breathing and a little perspiration from their pads, but is naturally balanced by the proper intake of fluid and food. On a daily basis, dogs should consume an amount of water that is roughly equivalent to their daily energy requirements expressed in calories; this is about 1.6 fl oz (50 ml) of water per 2.2 lbs (1 kg) of body weight. It's thus very important for a dog always to have access to a bowl of fresh, clean water and, when the dog has run around a lot, you should always have a bottle of water with which to quench its thirst and rehydrate it.

CARBOHYDRATES

Carbohydrates, although not strictly necessary for a dog, are often present in homemade diets, such as the recipes suggested in this book. There are two reasons for this. The first is an economic one: good-quality meat and fish are pricey, especially if you have several dogs or a large dog, so the addition of carbohydrates can thus help reduce costs. The second is an evolutionary reason. Despite dogs being descended from wolves—whose diets don't include carbs—their evolution has been among humans. One consequence of this has been a physiological change in the way dogs digest—they have adapted to eating carbohydrates and cereals, the cornerstone of the human diet over thousands of years. This evolution has not, however, affected all breeds in the same way; those that have been domesticated for longer (for example, the Saluki) have a better ability to make use of carbohydrates than breeds that have been domesticated more recently (for example, the Siberian Husky, the Weimaraner, and the Czechoslovakian Wolfdog).

The main type of carbohydrate that is digestible for dogs is starch, which is found in cereals such as rice, pasta and bread, root vegetables (potatoes and tapioca), and legumes (peas and green beans). As mentioned earlier, it takes dogs longer than humans to digest starch, only becoming a good source of energy if the foods that contain it have been cooked for a long time.

FIBER

Fiber, although hardly digestible, is an essential component of a dog's diet. The addition of foods that are high in fiber does, in fact, improve the health of the animal's gastrointestinal system, but it doesn't stop there. Its presence increases the volume of the meal; an excellent solution for overweight dogs, those that have been neutered, or senior dogs who need less calorie-rich food. Also, it's been proven that fiber plays an important role in the management of diseases such as diabetes and bacteria-borne illnesses of the intestines.

It should be stressed that there are two main types of fiber: soluble and insoluble. The former is able to absorb free water in the intestines (and is useful if a dog has diarrhea), and is fermented, at least in part, by intestinal microflora and stimulates the growth of beneficial bacteria and nourishes intestinal cells. The latter, on the other hand, can absorb very little water. It can't be assimilated by the dog but it helps to stimulate intestinal movement and can therefore help in the case of constipation.

The main sources of fiber are: wholegrains, legumes (green beans and peas in particular), apples (preferably with the skin left on), and vegetables, especially leafy greens; bran is also excellent, but is only recommended in cases of obesity because it is very high in insoluble fiber. To sum up, remember that, in theory, adding high amounts of fiber to your dog's food is not recommended because it can make it less appetizing, and also because the more soluble fiber sources can lead to diarrhea or flatulence.

HOW MANY ESSENTIAL NUTRIENTS SHOULD BE CONSUMED?

The recommended essential nutrients don't stay the same throughout a dog's life but vary depending on its physiological stages and following pathological disorders. The parameters used to balance the recipes in this book follow the minimum requirements related to the different essential nutrients established by FEDIAF (The European Pet Food Industry Federation). It is important to specify this because, among the various international bodies that exist, there is no unanimity on this point. In fact, depending on which source is consulted—FEDIAF; AAFCO (Association of American Feed Control Officials, USA); NRC (American Feed Control Officials, USA), NRC (National Research Council, USA/Canada), to name the most well-known— there are differences.

BASIC NUTRITIONAL REQUIREMENTS

Among the various international bodies there's no unanimity on the minimum nutritional requirements for a properly balanced diet for dogs. The reason for this difference is that while FEDIAF and AAFCO are concerned with pinpointing the data to meet the nutritional needs of healthy dogs (mainly based on commercially produced dog food), the NRC bases its data on nutrient-based scientific studies also.

This can lead to significant differences. An excellent example is that of the minimum protein requirement of a meal, which, according to NRC, is 10 percent DMB, and to FEDIAF is 18 percent DMB. The difference has arisen because the NRC considers only the essential amino acids; in nature, however, there are no foods that contain only these nutrients, just foods that contain some essential amino acids and some non-essential ones.

It is logical that FEDIAF's recommendation regarding the recommended minimum protein requirement is much higher. The reason for this difference is that while FEDIAF and AAFCO are concerned with pinpointing the data to meet the nutritional needs of healthy dogs with a food-based approach, NRC bases its data on nutrients-based approach, not on food *per se*.

BASIC NUTRITIONAL REQUIREMENTS

Toxic Foods

One of the most important things to be aware of when feeding
your dog a homemade diet is that some foods—normally ones
that are ever-present in our kitchens—and integral parts of our
daily diets, are poisonous to dogs and must never be given to
them. Of course, there are a few foods that are dangerous for
all dogs' health, and should always be avoided. A classic example
that everyone knows of is chocolate, which can cause reactions
such as vomiting and seizures, but listed below are other
ingredients to watch out for. These are just the most common
ingredients—for more information, speak to your veterinarian.

ONIONS, GARLIC, AND OTHER ALLIUMS

Onions (*Allium cepa*), garlic (*Allium Sativum*), leeks (*Allium
Porrum*), and chives (*Allium schoenoprasum*) are all plants
belonging to the Allium genus and contain sulfurous substances
that lead to gastrointestinal disorders and anemia in dogs.
Cooking or dehydrating them makes no difference in this, so
these ingredients must never be part of your pet's meal. The
most common signs of a dog's allergic reaction to these are
weakness, exhaustion, abdominal pain, vomiting and loss of
appetite, and may take place from one to several days after
the above plants have been ingested. If dogs ingest 15–30 g
of these plants per 2.2 lb (1 kg) of body weight, it is enough to
cause an alteration in their red blood cells. Some breeds of are
especially susceptible: for example, for Akita Inus and Shiba
Inus, just small amounts of these plants can trigger severe
reactions.

ETHANOL (ALCOHOL)

Ethanol intoxication is linked to the accidental ingestion
of alcoholic beverages and within one hour the dog develops
neurological symptoms, vomiting, dehydration and hypothermia.
Although these reactions may be very similar to those that
occur in humans, the amount necessary to cause intoxication
is significantly lower. The ingestion of rotten fruit should also
be avoided, because as it ferments, high levels of ethanol (alcohol)
are produced.

GRAPES

Another food to avoid giving to dogs is grapes, even after being cooked, fresh or dried, i.e. raisins or sultanas, or in the form of pomace (skins). In this case, kidney damage is a risk; the signs are vomiting, diarrhea, exhaustion, increased thirst and the amount of urine produced or, conversely, an absence of urine. The toxic principle and the exact mechanism of the toxicity have not yet been established in this case. In part, this is because cases have been reported where dogs have ingested 2.2 lbs (1 kg) of raisins and that this has had no effect on them, while other dogs have died after eating much smaller amounts.

HOPS

We are familiar with hops as a key ingredient in beer-making but, if swallowed by our dogs, hop flowers can lead to the development of malignant hyperthermia (a rapid rise in body temperature). Some breeds are prone to malignant hyperthermia even when they have not ingested hops (e.g. Greyhounds, Retrievers, Saint Bernards, Dobermans, Border Collies, northern breeds, etc.). Other signs of intoxication are vomiting, gasping, and dark brown urine.

MACADAMIA NUTS

As in the case of grapes, the mechanism of their toxicity is currently unknown and the dose required to induce toxicity has not been established precisely: in fact, there are known cases in which the toxic effects occurred after the ingestion of amounts of macadamia nuts, which range from 0.02 oz per 2 lb 2 oz (0.7 g per kg) of body weight to 2.2 oz per 2 lb 2 oz (62.4 g per kg). Signs usually appear within 12 hours of ingestion and include weakness, vomiting, and neurological symptoms.

CHOCOLATE, COFFEE, AND TEA

We humans often can't do without them, but for dogs, chocolate, coffee, and tea are extremely dangerous. Methylxanthines, active substances contained in all three of these foods (in the form of theobromine, caffeine, and theophylline respectively), are harmful if ingested by dogs as they lead to the appearance of neurological symptoms, cardiac stimulation, and the relaxation of smooth muscle. An amount of 20 mg of methylxanthine per kg of the dog's weight is sufficient to trigger these reactions. Dark chocolate is a commonly eaten product that has a high concentration of these substances and is, therefore, more dangerous, for example, than milk chocolate. The table below gives an idea of this concentration.

CAFFEINE	CONCENTRATION
Chocolate	2–40 mg/oz
Coffee	16–17 mg/oz
Coffee beans	280–570 mg/oz
Tea	20–90 mg/oz
Non-alcoholic beverages	5–7.5 mg/oz

THEOBROMINE	CONCENTRATION
White chocolate	0.25 mg/oz
Milk chocolate	44–60 mg/oz
Dark chocolate	135 mg/oz
Cocoa powder	400–737 mg/oz
Cacao beans	300–1500 mg/oz

AVOCADO

Another food that dogs should never eat is avocado, nor should they ingest any other part of the avocado tree (*Persea americana*). It is persine, a toxin with fungicidal action, that makes the tree toxic. This is what the tree has developed to defend itself from being attacked by mold. This substance is harmless to humans but harmful to several animals, dogs among them. Signs of avocado intoxication are vomiting, diarrhea, difficulty in breathing, heart problems and, in severe cases, it can lead to the death of the animal 12–24 hours after ingestion.

XYLITOL (ARTIFICIAL SWEETENER)

An artificial sweetener used in some food products labeled as 'sugar free' (chewing gum, candies, baked goods, etc.), xylitol is sold in powder form or as granules for normal domestic use. The effects it can have on a dog can be very serious as it is a strong stimulator of insulin release it can lead to severe hypoglycemia; in addition, ingesting xylitol has also been linked to severe liver damage in dogs. The quantity linked to liver damage is highly variable.

BREAD DOUGH

Although fresh bread does not lead to particular problems for dogs, ingesting raw dough, or raw leavened doughs of any kind, can be very dangerous. As soon as the yeast reaches the stomach of the animal, it ferments causing stomach distention; another consequence of fermentation is the production of ethanol which can cause further complications (see Ethanol).

TOXIC FOODS

Which Foods Lead to Allergic Reactions?

Some foods, despite not being toxic, can lead to health problems for dogs. As with humans, pets can develop allergies and intolerances to certain foods and, less often, to additives. Regarding allergies, adverse reactions affect the immune system. In fact, an allergy is an abnormal response by the immune system to the ingestion of a food normally tolerated by individuals of that species, no matter how much of it is eaten. The main signs of an allergy are itching or gastrointestinal problems that usually appear immediately after contact with the allergen, but which disappear within a few hours (although delayed reactions are possible). Only in the most severe cases will a food allergen lead to a reaction such as anaphylactic shock. To date, the extent of the problem related to allergies in dogs is still unclear; several scientists have tried to estimate a percentage of problems that have food as their origin, but so far the results haven't been unanimous. Regarding intolerances, an adverse reaction to a certain food does not involve the immune system to the same extent that a toxic food does.

LACTOSE

This is probably the most widespread example of dietary intolerance among dogs, but is certainly not the only one.

GLUTEN

Hereditary intolerance to gluten (the protein found in some cereals, including wheat, rye, and barley) should also be mentioned, but this is a problem that is rather limited in the veterinary field and only affects a small number of family lines of very few breeds.

HISTAMINE

One particular type of intolerance is that linked to histamine, a substance found in fish such as tuna and mackerel. Normally well tolerated, it can give rise to symptoms if it is present in high levels (as in the case of tuna and mackerel when past their best), or if the dog is on antibiotics (for example clavulanic acid) which inhibits the specific enzymes that digest this substance.

To identify the triggering factor of the possible adverse reaction your dog has undergone, the best thing is to follow an elimination diet. This is, ideally, a diet based on ingredients that the animal has never eaten and which excludes the foods that were normally given to it until then.

In this case, it is of great help if a homemade diet is already followed as you can be certain about how the dog's food was prepared and what exactly is in the meal; commercial dog food, in fact, often contains a small number of ingredients, sometimes hidden ones, which are used as sources of starch, fats or other nutrients. On the other hand, even in homemade food, it's necessary to pay close attention to the use of particular substances (such as commercial dietary supplements) that may be a source of hidden allergens, as can possible contamination from unwanted proteins while a meal is being prepared.

A Note on Special Diets

We all know how our own food choices can be influenced by passing trends, the occasional popularity of a particular ingredient, or the results of scientific research—the same goes for homemade dog diets. Sometimes, a certain diet can end up in the limelight and spark curiosity, especially if it concerns "healthier" or "more suitable" food. The following are some of the diets that have recently gained traction in both homemade meals and industrial ones based on specially designed kibble: the BARF diet, the Paleo diet, the Grain-Free or Low-Carb diet, and Vegan and Vegetarian diets. In general, these are diets that limit or eliminate one or more types of nutrients from meals, and so must therefore be evaluated and adjusted by your veterinarian or veterinary nutritionist. You can use these descriptions as a starting point for further reading, should you wish to investigate further.

THE BARF DIET

Coined in 1993 by an Australian veterinarian, one of the most common homemade diets is BARF (Biologically Appropriate Raw Food). The main premise of the diet is to recreate the typical diet of a carnivorous predator (in this case, a dog) in nature; it is, therefore, mainly composed of meat, offal, and meaty bones—all totally raw.

There's also a certain amount of fruit and vegetables added, but cereals are usually excluded (sources of starch such as peas or potatoes are very occasionally included). The daily portion of food for a BARF diet is calculated based on the weight of your dog and comes to around 2 percent to 4 percent of its weight, depending on its age and physical condition. The quantity of food required given must be as follows: 70–80 percent ingredients of animal origin and 20–30 percent of plant origin.

This diet is considered to be good for the digestive system, and to the physical requirements of dogs, because the focus is on their historic preditory nature; their diet—before their encounter with man—did not contain cereals, and so starch was not part of it. Bascially, the domestication of dogs has meant that their diets have been adapted to suit ours, which means having an intake of carbohydrates and cereals—this is now considered to be all part of a complete and balanced canine diet.

Among the advantages of this diet are glossier fur, elements of better oral hygiene, and improved digestion. So in this instance, the presence of bones in a dog's diet helps to keep its teeth clean, and the use of raw bones—that are harder—limits problems caused by breaking or splintering. However, as discussed earlier in the book, the consumption of bones is never risk free, as splinters can still occur with raw bones—therefore, it's advisable to always use bone meal instead.

With regard to better digestion, the BARF diet—that is grain free and thus suitable for dogs who show an adverse reaction to starches (in particular the Czechoslovakian Wolfdog, the Saarloos Wolfdog and Weimaraner)—can be a boon (even though, to be fair, it has never been proven that a starch-free homemade "cooked" diet is not just as beneficial in cases such as these).

Then there is the matter of vitamins and minerals. The BARF diet is considered, by those who champion it, to be a complete diet that is able to satisfy a dog's requirements and thus does not include dietary supplements. In effect, this type of food given to dogs is not real prey; in other words, animals that roam free in the wild. It is clearly stretching it a bit to think that a farmed chicken (slaughtered when it is about a month old) that has, moreover, been skinned, plucked and gutted, can be nutritionally compared to a bird that has lived for a few years in the wild. Even the role played by the vitamins and minerals in fruit, vegetables, seeds and herbs is also often overestimated.

Let's take a closer look at what is at the core of this diet; the use of raw meat. Recent studies related to a number of ingredients—sold specifically for the BARF diet—and which contain meat, bones and by-products of beef, poultry, ducks, lamb, and horses, and are well-known brands sold in supermarkets, specialized stores and by veterinarians, have been proven to contain levels of Escherichia coli in concentrations higher than those considered dangerous for humans; two other dangerous parasites have also been found: Sarcocystis cruzi and Toxoplasma gondii, not to mention Listeria and Salmonella. It is common knowledge that raw meat can be contaminated by viruses (e.g. Aujeszky's), bacteria and parasites (E. coli and Salmonella, for example, are bacteria found in raw chicken and turkey meat) by which, it has to be said, dogs are less affected than we are, but it is also true that bacterial toxins are fairly common, in particular affecting animals that are immunodeficient or suffer from gastrointestinal illnesses. We may be the owners of the dogs but, in this case, we are more exposed to the problem. In fact, we can come into contact with these bacteria when handling or incorrectly storing raw meat for our dog's food, and it does not stop there: our dog can contaminate our home environment if its fur comes into contact with feces, or humans pick up feces, and contaminate areas where their dog defecates. The Food and Drug Administration (FDA) thus also recommends keeping ingredients used for a BARF diet separate from other foods, storing them immediately in the freezer if not all of them are needed, and disinfecting all utensils that come into contact with raw meat every time they are used.

THE PALEO DIET

A good number of the observations made here so far—and that are related to the current BARF diet trend—also analyze other diets that should be taken into consideration, starting with the Paleo diet, which has many aspects that are common to the BARF diet. First of all is the principle that inspires it; the wish to feed one's dog in a way that is more in line with its nature as a predator. The Paleo diet takes its name from the kind of diet people had during the Paleolithic Age that was based on fishing, hunting and the gathering of wild plants. Transposed to the animal world, the wolf is used as a model as it does not put on weight, lives a long and active life, and finds everything it needs in the wild. Supporters of the Paleo diet believe that little has changed over thousands of years in the digestive system and in the physical predisposition of dogs—this goes for humans, too—and so, a return to a "caveman" diet can only be good for our health and well being and that of our four-legged friends. With a similar raison d'être to the BARF diet, the Paleo diet is also grain and dairy free.

There are, however, two fundamental differences between one diet and the other: the BARF diet relates to the non-cooking of food, and the Paleo diet to the absence of bones.

Unlike with the BARF diet, the Paleo diet allows various types of meat (pork is always cooked), fruits and vegetables to be cooked. Food should not, however, be cooked for a long time and, above all, it should never be mixed in a bowl that has contained raw food. In addition, the two meals should be spaced apart with more time than usual between them to avoid any problems stemming from the different length of time it takes for digestion to take place. According to supporters of the Paleo diet, raw food is easier and faster to digest than cooked food but this has never been scientifically proven. The above-mentioned factors and precautions are also valid when using raw meat.

As for meaty bones, these are not included in the Paleo diet, thus avoiding the problem of possible cuts to your dog's mouth, broken teeth, and injuries to its intestines. The lack of nutrients such as calcium and other salts can be compensated by dietary supplements such as bone meal or powdered eggshells. Natural dietary supplements such as herbs and spices can often also

A NOTE ON SPECIAL DIETS

DIET IN DETAIL

be used to compensate the lack of nutrients linked to the afore-mentioned impracticality of feeding your dog actual prey from the wild.

In this case too, as it is for a grain-free diet, the diet is suitable for animals that have adverse reactions to starches.

A GRAIN-FREE OR LOW-CARB DIET

A grain-free or cereal-free diet is in line with the idea that a dog's digestive system is unsuited to digesting grains. As its name suggests, grains and cereals—corn and wheat, in particular—have been eliminated from this diet. Variations on the low-carb diet include adding oats, millet and brown rice that have better glycemic load and so are more suitable for our pets. Grain free does not mean that the diet does not include carbohydrates as some people mistakenly believe—thinking that, as dogs are carnivores, they do not need carbs—as it does in fact include potatoes, peas and tapioca, as well as ingredients such as buckwheat and quinoa. In general, low-carb diets are higher in protein that grain-free ones.

One of the main reasons people choose this kind of diet for their pets is the belief that it can improve the health of dogs with allergies or intolerances. On the one hand, cereals are not the most common allergens to be found in food for dogs but, on the other, it is true that the most effective way of identifying the trigger factor of an adverse reaction is an exclusion diet. Once the trigger factor has been singled out, a dog's diet can then be reformulated using this knowledge but without necessarily eliminating all other cereals and grains as well. When it comes to coeliacs, as has already been mentioned, this is not a major problem in the veterinary field and it only affects a few family lines of a limited number of breeds. Furthermore, a gluten-free diet—necessary for coeliacs—does not have to be a grain-free diet as there are gluten-free cereals that can be included in the diet of a coeliac dog.

As already stated with regard to the BARF and Paleo diets, the premise is that diets from which cereals are excluded can be suitable for the requirements of dogs who have adverse reactions to starches.

We now come to the fundamental component of this type of diet; proteins, whose presence is particularly high (38–45 percent). As we have seen, and to avoid any negative consequences, the nutritional requirements of a dog must be carefully evaluated in accordance with many factors, starting from the stage of life it is at and the amount of daily activity it does.

Grain-free diets are not recommended during the growth stage because a puppy's gastrointestinal system is still immature and needs more easily digested carbohydrates than those provided by root vegetables and legumes. Limiting carbohydrates means that protein and phosphorus content are higher and so low-carb diets should be avoided for dogs with kidney problems.

If you opt for a grain-free or low-carb diet, it is normal that your dog will appear to be less sated immediately after a meal: this is because the glycemic peak from root vegetables and legumes is not as immediate but, the advantage is that satiety lasts longer.

A VEGETARIAN OR VEGAN DIET

If the diets mentioned here highlight the carnivorous nature of dogs, vegetarian and vegan diets go in a completely different direction. This view is totally overturned with the basic idea that dogs, after thousands of years of living with humans, have lost their purely carnivorous ways and can now be considered omnivores. In this case, the choice is mainly an ethical one; if you love animals, it is logical that a difference is not made between pets and those that are "acceptable" to eat. Moreover, reasons closely linked to health are given, and these are mainly to do with the quality of the meat given to dogs: at the heart of the matter is the way in which animals are intensively farmed, the use of antibiotics, and the unhygienic conditions that these animals for food are subjected to.

So, what are the foods that are part of a vegetarian or vegan diet? Broadly speaking, and just as with a human diet, a canine vegetarian diet does not include meat and fish but is open to other animal proteins (for example, a lacto-ovo-vegetarian diet includes milk, cheese, yogurt, and eggs), while a vegan diet excludes all animal and animal-derived proteins. The main sources of vegetable protein in both of these cases are legumes (soy in particular), whole grains, wheat germ, and seeds such as sunflower and sesame seeds. To obtain meals that are as complete and balanced as possible, varieties of nuts, sprouts, seaweed, cereal by-products, tofu, fruit and vegetables are added depending on their specific nutritional characteristics. To compensate for any deficiencies, ingredients such as yeast or yeast extract (Marmite, for instance) are used to make some foods more appetizing as well as enriching them with B vitamins; raw seed oils are also used as a source of essential fatty acids. Don't forget that dogs need hard food to chew on to keep their jaws and gums healthy; raw carrots or whole apples can be given to them for this purpose. In general, it is a good idea to carefully evaluate the presence of nutrients such as amino acids (taurine, methionine, lysine, tryptophan), minerals (calcium, phosphorus, zinc), vitamins (group B, D3, A and E) and fats (linoleic acid, EPA, DHA), deficiencies of which can result in various diseases.

Remember, however, that although the digestive systems of dogs have altered because of their close relationship with humans, morphologically they are still omnivores and their gastrointestinal tract is shorter and contains digestive enzymes and intestinal microbes that are different from those of herbivores. So, to properly satisfy your dog's nutritional requirements, a vegan or vegetarian diet must be balanced and integrated with great care. In addition to being less digestible than a "carnivorous" diet, one of the most common problems can be a deficiency of vitamin B12 (found in food of animal origin), the first symptoms of which are a general weakness and a loss of fur, but these can be overcome with specific dietary supplements. A dog's amino-acid requirements are higher than those of omnivorous animals so, given that a vegan diet limits some amino acids (although they are present in small quantities), they must nevertheless be made up for. In general, and to ensure that your dog's nutritional requirements are always met, specific blood tests are recommended. In addition, special attention should be paid to any abnormal behavior or signs of discomfort and, should these arise, immediately consult your veterinarian.

Given the problems linked to the absence of animal proteins, these kinds of diet are not recommended for puppies, pregnant or nursing dogs, or senior dogs that have very specific requirements and are less able to adapt to a change in diet.

A vegetarian or vegan diet can be recommended in cases where there is a need to eliminate proteins of animal origin, as for example in dogs with a genetic predisposition to urinary stones (Dalmatians, Bulldogs).

DOGS AND ENTOMOPHAGY

The need to guarantee a source of protein for a world population that will rise to over 9 billion by 2050 has forced us to take a closer look at using insects as a source of animal protein for humans as well as animals. Insects are a more efficient source of protein and amino acids than other creatures traditionally farmed for human food and animal feed: the same amount of protein produced requires infinitely smaller quantities of feed, clean water and land, not to mention that greenhouse-gas emissions are lower.

Eating insects, furthermore, is nothing new. The FAO has confirmed that insects are currently part of the diet of about two billion people (just under one third of the world's entire population) and have been part of the human diet since prehistoric times.

Studies conducted on dogs—feeding them the larvae of the species Hermetia illucens as a source of protein—showed that they are able to digest and assimilate proteins from insects and that these proteins could be a suitable and digestible source of protein with a biological value (amount of essential amino acids) comparable to that of meat (see Bibliography, page 219).

The idea that our dogs can shift towards consuming larvae meal made from insects—raw materials that are already available on the market in several European countries—should not be dismissed.

A NOTE ON SPECIAL DIETS

DIET IN DETAIL

Disclaimer

All the recipes in this book are suitable for healthy dogs. This means that they provide all the nutrients that your dog needs so that its nutritional requirements are met, but they are not intended as diets for animals with specific illnesses, for which a veterinary nutritionist should always be consulted.

Each recipe must be followed to the letter and ingredients must not be swapped. You should also bear in mind that the chemical composition of raw materials may not be the same in every country: to guarantee minimal variation from the original and ensure the correct balance of the recipe, we recommend that you always use the type of ingredients specified in the recipe, in particular with regard the weight and age of your dog.

Changing from commercial food to homemade food must always be done gradually to avoid gastrointestinal problems. If any complication of this nature arises, consult a veterinary nutritionist.

Quantities are expressed in grams and imperial measurements for individual ingredients to make both 2 lb 2 oz/1 kg of food as well as daily portions and are the result of mathematical calculations. For convenience, you can round quantities up or down but never more than 10 percent. The recipe will still be properly balanced.

The nutritional values of the raw materials used in the recipes of this book come from two sources: one German (https://www.sfk.online/#/home); and the other Italian (http://nut.entecra.it/636/banche_dati.html).

A NOTE ON BREEDS AND PORTION SIZES

Each portion of food meets the daily nutritional requirements of a neutered dog, however, there are one or two exceptions. In the case of unneutered dogs, the quantities should be increased by 20%. In the case of breeds that naturally tend to gain weight, such as Retrievers and Nordic dogs, portion sizes should be reduced by 20%. If these dogs are unneutered, however, follow the portion sizes given in the recipes. Finally, portions for neutered Greyhounds, Alani and Weimaraner should be increased by 20%.

Supplements

Although varied and balanced, a dog's homemade diet must always include the use of supplements. These, in fact, are essential to fill the various nutritional deficiencies, which derive from the loss of nutrients during cooking and the difficulty of administering bones and viscera in a daily and domestic context. It is true, in fact, that a prey-based diet could satisfy all the nutritional needs of an animal, but in our daily lives our pet does not have this availability. Furthermore, it would entail a greater risk of transmission of some serious infections for humans, such as Salmonellosis, Listeriosis, Campilobacteriosis, etc.

The supplement we suggest to use is Balance IT®, available online and from veterinarians and nutritionists. In most cases this is the only supplement needed for all dishes; an additional supplement—True Nutrition Vegan Protein Formula—provides essential amino acids for some vegan and vegetarian dishes.

If however, you are based in Europe, it might be easier to source an alternative to Balance IT®, more commonly available, such as the Completa Q.Diet®, which in most cases is used alone to balance the recipes. If you need to swap out Balance IT® for Completa Q. Diet® or find Trovet Balance, VMP Zoetis® and IDA Plus Barf Vitamins Liquid® easier to source, please refer to the conversion table below.

Balance IT®	=	Completa Q.diet ®
2 g		1.5 g
4 g		3 g
6 g		4.5 g
8 g		6 g
10 g		7.5 g
12 g		9 g
14 g		10.5 g
16 g		12 g
18 g		13.5 g
20 g		15 g

Balance IT®	=	Trovet Balance	+	VMP Zoetis ®	+	IDA Plus Barf Vitamins Liquids ®
2.5 g		2.5 g		¼ cpr		0.75 ml
5 g		5 g		½ cpr		1.5 ml
7.5 g		7.5 g		¾ cpr		2.25 ml
10 g		10 g		1 cpr		3 ml
12.5 g		12.5 g		1 + ¼ cprs		3.75 ml
15 g		15 g		1 + ½ cprs		4.5 ml
17.5 g		17.5 g		1 + ¾ cprs		5.25 ml
20 g		20 g		2 cprs		6 g

A Note from the Author

The origins of humans' friendships with dogs go back through the mists of time. The first encounter can be traced back to a period of time ranging from about 30,000 years ago, when some species of wolves approached human communities, establishing a mutually advantageous relationship with them. And so it was that *Canis lupus* began transforming into *Canis familiaris*, guaranteeing protection for humans against attacks from other predators and receiving, in exchange, the certainty of a meal that consisted, in the main, of the scraps from human meals. This represented a crucial step in the evolution of dogs, both from a social, as well as a physiological, perspective. Unlike the wolf, dogs are now, to all intents and purposes, accepted as family members, and their digestive systems have developed differently, when compared to those of their ancestors. This gap has been still further accentuated by the genetic selection that humans have conducted, over time, that has led to there now being 400 identifiable breeds of dog.

From a purely dietary standpoint, it could be said that more than 10,000 years of living alongside humans have gradually made dogs more similar to their masters. That is to say, they have led dogs have adapted to a diet rich in carbohydrates and cereals, historically pivotal in human evolution, but excluded from the diets of wolves in their wild state. Various scientists have demonstrated that there are three genes which have evolved in dogs during domestication, and these are involved in starch digestion and glucose uptake, providing dogs with a certain capacity to assimilate carbohydrate. This change, however, did not occur in equal measure for all breeds, but it is particularly noticeable in those that have been tame for longer (more so in Salukis than in Siberian Huskies, for example). The processes of domestication and genetic selection, have, on the other hand, had no effect on other metabolic tracts. This means that dogs have developed anatomical functional and digestive features, that are altogether singular, and they cannot be included in the classical categories of carnivores (of which cats are a part) or omnivores. That said, what is clear, is just how important it is to know and understand dogs' real needs and their actual nutritional requirements in order to provide them with a healthy and complete diet.

The management of dogs' meals is very delicate, even from a social point of view, and it directly affects the relationship between dogs and families. Despite having co-habited with humans for thousands of years, dogs continue to apply ancestral dynamics to food and give their meal a key role in defining the hierarchical relationships with their owners. Impromptu management, i.e. owners giving dogs snacks, rewards, part of their own meal, or leftovers, can have negative consequences, not just on their health but also their behavioral patterns.

This choice of feeding a dog with a homemade diet implies paying special attention to needs, nutrients, times, and methods of providing food, involving dogs' owners in the preparation of the meal, not just from a practical but also an emotional point of view. In this sense, it can be said that preparing a meal for your dog contributes to strengthening still further the relationship of affection and friendship that ties owners to their dogs.

ABOUT THE AUTHOR

Liviana Prola is a research scientist at the Department of Veterinary Science at Turin University, Italy. A doctor of veterinary science, she also has a PhD in Animal Nutrition, is a diplomat at the European College of Veterinary and Comparative Nutrition, and runs a pet nutrition consultancy service for pet-food companies, vets, and animal owners. She is also president of the Italian Society of Animal Nutrition.

INDEX

Index

Acknowledgements

There are three people without whom this book would not have been possible.

- Prof. Pier Paolo Mussa for giving me an insight, in my first few years of university, how fascinating and exciting the science of nutrition could be, and how it could become, to all effects, a profession in its own right within Veterinary Medicine.

- Dr. Mario Agrillo, for helping me to progress with new concepts. I cannot thank him enough for supporting me when it comes to following my intuition, for stopping me taking any wrong turns, and above all, for having reviewed step-by-step, each and every recipe in these pages.

- Finally, I would like to thank Giulia Malerba for her patience and assiduousness in her assistance on this project.

Bibliography

Association of American Feed Control Officials. Official Publication. Oxford, IN: Association of Feed Control Officials, 2010.

Axelsson E., Ratnakumar A., Arendt M.L., et al. (2013) *The genomic signature of dog domestication reveals adaptation to a starch-rich diet.* Nature 495, 360–364.

Bauer J.E. (2007) *Responses of dogs to dietary omega-3 fatty acids.* J Am Vet Med Assoc 231, 1657–1661.

Bosch G., Hagen-Plantinga E., Hendriks W.H. (2015) *Dietary nutrient profiles of wild wolves: insights for optimal dog nutrition?* British Journal of Nutrition, 113, S40–S54.

Boyko A.R., Quignon P., Li L., et al. (2010) *A simple genetic architecture underlies morphological variation in dogs.* PLoS Biol 8, e1000451.

Clutton-Brock J. (1995) *Origins of the dog: domestication and early history.* In *The Domestic Dog: Its Evolution, Behaviour and Interactions with People.* pp. 7–20 (Serpell J., editor). Cambridge, UK: Cambridge University Press.

Commission Directive 2008/38/EC of 5 March 2008 establishing a list of intended uses of animal feedingstuffs for particular nutritional purposes.

Cortinovis C., Caloni F. (2016) *Housefold food items toxic to dogs and cats.* Front Vet Sci 22; 3: 26.

Driscoll C.A., MacDonald D.W. (2010) *Top dogs: wolf domestication and wealth.* J Biol 9, 10.

Driscoll C.A., Macdonald D.W., O'Brien S.J. (2009) *From wild animals to domestic pets, an evolutionary view of domestication.* Proc Natl Acad Sci U S A 106, 9971–9978.

European Pet Food Industry (FEDIAF). Nutritional guidelines for complete and complementary pet foods for cats and dogs, 2017.

Freedman A.H., Gronau I., Schweizer R.M., et al. (2014) *Genome sequencing highlights the dynamic early history of dogs.* PLoS Genet 10, e1004016.

Hand M.S., Thatcher C.D., Remillard R.L., et al. (editors) (2010) *Small Animal Clinical Nutrition.* 5th ed. Topeka, KS: Mark Morris Institute.

Hewson-Hughes A.K., Hewson-Hughes V.L., Colyer A., et al. (2013) *Consistent proportional macronutrient intake selected by adult domestic cats (Felis catus) despite variations in macronutrient and moisture content of foods offered.* J Comp Physiol B 183, 525–536.

Hewson-Hughes A.K., Hewson-Hughes V.L., Colyer A., et al. (2013) *Geometric analysis of macronutrient selection in breeds of the domestic dog, Canis lupus familiaris.* Behav Ecol 24, 293–304.

Mussa P.P., Prola L. (2005) *Dog nutrient requirements: new knowledge.* Vet Res Commun 29 (2): 35-38.

NRC (2006) *Nutrient Requirements of Dogs and Cats.* Washington, DC: National Academies Press.

Russo N., Vergnano D., Bergero D., Prola L. (2017) *Small pilot survey on parents' perception of the relationship between children and pets.* Vet Sci 16 (4)4.

Vilà C., Wayne R.K. (1999) *Hybridization between wolves and dogs.* Conserv Biol 13, 195–198.

VonHoldt B.M., Pollinger J.P., Lohmueller K.E., et al. (2010) *Genome-wide SNP and haplotype analyses reveal a rich history underlying dog domestication.* Nature 464, 898–902.

Phaidon Press Limited
Regent's Wharf
All Saints Street
London N1 9PA

Phaidon Press Inc.
65 Bleecker Street
New York, NY 10012

phaidon.com

First published 2018
© 2018 Phaidon Press Limited

ISBN 978 0 7148 7740 2

A CIP catalogue record for this book
is available from the British Library and
the Library of Congress.

Printed in China

Commissioning Editor: Emilia Terragni
Project Editor: Eve O'Sullivan
Production Controller: Lisa Fiske
Design: Julia Hasting
Illustration: Kevin Waldron
Artworking: Albino Tavares
Content management: Dalcò Edizioni Srl

Icon Credits
The Noun Project: Red Meat, Jeremie Sommet;
Poultry, Drumstick, Vectors Market; Vegetarian, Carrot,
Michał Czekała; Fish, Sina & Marie; Vegan, Sprout, H.A;
Grain Free, Madeleine Bennett; Energetic, Lightning
Bolt, Konstantinos Riginos; Game, Pine Tree, Mohamed
Amine Benzakour; Light, Leaf, iejank; Tennis ball, Anton
Gridz; Dog collar, Delsart Olivia; Heart, Angelina Fara;
Dog collar, Denora Daujatas; Paw, Sridharan S; Beach
Ball, Anbileru Adaleru.

The publisher would like to thank Theresa
Bebbington, Paola Binaghi, Vanessa Bird, Marge
Chandler, David Devonport, Sophie Elletson, Giulia
Malerba, Margherita Scorletti, and Gregor Shepherd.